THE CAMBRIDGE BIBLE COMMENTARY

NEW ENGLISH BIBLE

GENERAL EDITORS

P. R. ACKROYD, A. R. C. LEANEY,
J. W. PACKER

PROVERBS

THE BOOK OF
PROVERBS

COMMENTARY BY

R. N. WHYBRAY

*Reader in Theology in the
University of Hull*

CAMBRIDGE
AT THE UNIVERSITY PRESS
1972

Published by the Syndics of the Cambridge University Press
Bentley House, 200 Euston Road, London NW1 2DB
American Branch: 32 East 57th Street, New York, N.Y.10022

© Cambridge University Press 1972

Library of Congress Catalogue Card Number: 70-171687

ISBNS:
0 521 08364 8 hard covers
0 521 09679 0 paperback

Printed in Great Britain
at the University Printing House, Cambridge
(Brooke Crutchley, University Printer)

GENERAL EDITORS' PREFACE

The aim of this series is to provide the text of the New English Bible closely linked to a commentary in which the results of modern scholarship are made available to the general reader. Teachers and young people have been especially kept in mind. The commentators have been asked to assume no specialized theological knowledge, and no knowledge of Greek and Hebrew. Bare references to other literature and multiple references to other parts of the Bible have been avoided. Actual quotations have been given as often as possible.

The completion of the New Testament part of the series in 1967 provides a basis upon which the production of the much larger Old Testament and Apocrypha series can be undertaken. The welcome accorded to the series has been an encouragement to the editors to follow the same general pattern, and an attempt has been made to take account of criticisms which have been offered. One necessary change is the inclusion of the translators' footnotes since in the Old Testament these are more extensive, and essential for the understanding of the text.

Within the severe limits imposed by the size and scope of the series, each commentator will attempt to set out the main findings of recent biblical scholarship and to describe the historical background to the text. The main theological issues will also be critically discussed.

Much attention has been given to the form of the volumes. The aim is to produce books each of which will be read consecutively from first to last page. The introductory material leads naturally into the text, which itself leads into the alternating sections of the commentary.

The series is accompanied by three volumes of a more general character. *Understanding the Old Testament* sets out to provide the larger historical and archaeological background, to say something about the life and thought of the people of the Old Testament, and to answer the question 'Why should we study the Old Testament?'. *The Making of the Old Testament* is concerned with the formation of the books of the Old Testament and Apocrypha in the context of the ancient near eastern world, and with the ways in which these books have come down to us in the life of the Jewish and Christian communities. *Old Testament Illustrations* contains maps, diagrams and photographs with an explanatory text. These three volumes are designed to provide material helpful to the understanding of the individual books and their commentaries, but they are also prepared so as to be of use quite independently.

P. R. A.
A. R. C. L.
J. W. P.

CONTENTS

The footnotes to the N.E.B. text   *page* ix

❋ ❋ ❋ ❋ ❋ ❋ ❋ ❋ ❋ ❋ ❋ ❋ ❋

Introduction   1

The wisdom tradition in the ancient Near East   3

The book of Proverbs and its models: resemblances and differences   7

The structure of the book   12

How to read the book   12

❋ ❋ ❋ ❋ ❋ ❋ ❋ ❋ ❋ ❋ ❋ ❋ ❋

Advice to the reader   15

Wisdom and folly contrasted   46

A collection of wise sayings   56

Thirty wise sayings   126

Other collections of wise sayings   144

A capable wife   182

❋ ❋ ❋ ❋ ❋ ❋ ❋ ❋ ❋ ❋ ❋ ❋ ❋

List of subjects   187

❋ ❋ ❋ ❋ ❋ ❋ ❋ ❋ ❋ ❋ ❋ ❋ ❋

A NOTE ON FURTHER READING   189

INDEX   191

THE FOOTNOTES TO THE
N.E.B. TEXT

The footnotes to the N.E.B. text are designed to help the reader
either to understand particular points of detail – the meaning of a
name, the presence of a play upon words – or to give information
about the actual text. Where the Hebrew text appears to be erroneous,
or there is doubt about its precise meaning, it may be necessary to
turn to manuscripts which offer a different wording, or to ancient
translations of the text which may suggest a better reading, or to
offer a new explanation based upon conjecture. In such cases, the
footnotes supply very briefly an indication of the evidence, and
whether the solution proposed is one that is regarded as possible or
as probable. Various abbreviations are used in the footnotes.

(1) Some abbreviations are simply of terms used in explaining a
point: *ch(s)*., chapter(s); *cp*., compare; *lit*., literally; *mng*., meaning;
MS(S)., manuscript(s), i.e. Hebrew manuscript(s), unless otherwise
stated; *om*., omit(s); *or*, indicating an alternative interpretation; *poss*.,
possible; *prob*., probable; *rdg*., reading.

(2) Other abbreviations indicate sources of information from which
better interpretations or readings may be obtained.

Aq. Aquila, a Greek translator of the Old Testament (perhaps
about A.D. 130) characterized by great literalness.

Aram. Aramaic – may refer to the text in this language (used in
parts of Ezra and Daniel), or to the meaning of an Aramaic word.
Aramaic belongs to the same language family as Hebrew, and is
known from about 1000 B.C. over a wide area of the Middle East,
including Palestine.

Heb. Hebrew – may refer to the Hebrew text or may indicate the
literal meaning of the Hebrew word.

Josephus Flavius Josephus (A.D. 37/8–about 100), author of the *Jewish
Antiquities*, a survey of the whole history of his people, directed
partly at least to a non-Jewish audience, and of various other works,
notably one on the *Jewish War* (that of A.D. 66–73) and a defence
of Judaism (*Against Apion*).

Luc. Sept. Lucian's recension of the Septuagint, an important edition
made in Antioch in Syria about the end of the third century A.D.

Pesh. Peshitta or Peshitto, the Syriac version of the Old Testament. Syriac is the name given chiefly to a form of Eastern Aramaic used by the Christian community. The translation varies in quality, and is at many points influenced by the Septuagint or the Targums.

Sam. Samaritan Pentateuch – the form of the first five books of the Old Testament as used by the Samaritan community. It is written in Hebrew in a special form of the Old Hebrew script, and preserves an important form of the text, somewhat influenced by Samaritan ideas.

Scroll(s) Scroll(s), commonly called the Dead Sea Scrolls, found at or near Qumran from 1947 onwards. These important manuscripts shed light on the state of the Hebrew text as it was developing in the last centuries B.C. and the first century A.D.

Sept. Septuagint (meaning 'seventy'; often abbreviated as the Roman numeral LXX), the name given to the main Greek version of the Old Testament. According to tradition, the Pentateuch was translated in Egypt in the third century B.C. by 70 (or 72) translators, six from each tribe, but the precise nature of its origin and development is not fully known. It was intended to provide Greek-speaking Jews with a convenient translation. Subsequently it came to be much revered by the Christian community.

Symm. Symmachus, another Greek translator of the Old Testament (beginning of the third century A.D.), who tried to combine literalness with good style. Both Lucian and Jerome viewed his version with favour.

Targ. Targum, a name given to various Aramaic versions of the Old Testament, produced over a long period and eventually standardized, for the use of Aramaic-speaking Jews.

Theod. Theodotion, the author of a revision of the Septuagint (probably second century A.D.), very dependent on the Hebrew text.

Vulg. Vulgate, the most important Latin version of the Old Testament, produced by Jerome about A.D. 400, and the text most used throughout the Middle Ages in western Christianity.

[...] In the text itself square brackets are used to indicate probably late additions to the Hebrew text.

(Fuller discussion of a number of these points may be found in *The Making of the Old Testament* in this series)

THE BOOK OF

PROVERBS

✳ ✳ ✳ ✳ ✳ ✳ ✳ ✳ ✳ ✳ ✳ ✳ ✳

INTRODUCTION

Every language has its own popular proverbs and sayings
which enrich and enliven ordinary speech. 'The early bird
catches the worm'; 'A stitch in time saves nine'; 'Too many
cooks spoil the broth' – these are characteristic examples of
English proverbs; most of us can think of many more. They
represent the accumulated experience of a people and express
it in a brief and memorable form. Among uneducated people
especially they function as a rough and ready philosophy and a
set of practical rules, and are handed down from one generation to another. 'Spare the rod and spoil the child', for example, has served through many generations as a rudimentary
educational theory.

Ancient Israel was no exception. The Old Testament contains a number of popular proverbs and sayings not unlike
our own, for example, 'Like mother, like daughter' (Ezek.
16: 44); 'One wrong begets another' (1 Sam. 24: 13); 'The
lame must not think himself a match for the nimble'
(1 Kings 20: 11).

At first sight Proverbs, especially certain sections like 10:
1–22: 16; 25–9, which consist mainly of large numbers of short
sayings with no apparent arrangement or connection between
them, might seem to be simply a collection of such popular
sayings; but this is not so. For one thing, there are far too
many of them. The essence of a popular saying is that it is
common property, familiar to everyone. But there are far too
many sayings in Proverbs for this to have been so. Most of us
would find it difficult to remember more than a few dozen

I

English proverbs. No people could have had at their fingertips a vast collection like this.

Closer inspection confirms this judgement. These 'proverbs' differ in many ways from popular proverbs and sayings. The popular proverb is a short, pithy, memorable saying in prose. But the sayings in Proverbs are in poetry. They are also of a more literary character: they strive for effect rather than for memorability, using elaborate phraseology which goes far beyond the making of a simple point. Compare, for example, the simplicity of the popular sayings 'Like mother, like daughter' and 'One wrong begets another' with the following:

> Like apples of gold set in silver filigree
> is a word spoken in season. (25: 11)

> Like a golden earring or a necklace of Nubian gold
> is a wise man whose reproof finds attentive ears.
> (25: 12)

> The wise man has his home full of fine and costly
> treasures;
> the stupid man is a mere spendthrift. (21: 20)

One can hardly imagine such sentences forming the common stock of sayings of the ordinary man.

It is also important to notice that many of the sayings in Proverbs are concerned with circumstances entirely outside the experience of the ordinary man. 16: 15, for example, would have meaning only for the small number of people who had regular access to the king:

> In the light of the king's countenance is life,
> his favour is like a rain-cloud in the spring.

It is true that some of the sayings in Proverbs may have been composed on the basis of simpler, popular sayings. For example, in 24:5 the first half ('Wisdom prevails over strength') may have been a popular saying which has been given a more literary appearance by the addition of the second line ('knowledge over brute force'). But this is unlikely to be true of more than a few. It is difficult to avoid the conclusion that most of the sayings in Proverbs are literary creations whose authors had a high degree of education. And this is obviously true of the longer poems – especially in chapters 1–9 – which also form part of Proverbs.

THE WISDOM TRADITION IN THE ANCIENT NEAR EAST

The culture of ancient Israel was not a unique phenomenon but belonged to a much wider cultural tradition shared by the neighbouring peoples, especially Egypt, Mesopotamia and Syria. Israel was a latecomer to the community of nations, and so became heir to a culture which had already flourished for many centuries. It is therefore important to look at the literature of the ancient Near East for clues to the origin of the types of literature which we find in Proverbs. Fortunately a great deal of this literature has come to light during the last 150 years.

One of the types of Egyptian and Mesopotamian literature is that which modern scholars call 'wisdom literature'. Most of this is much older than any part of the Old Testament. In Egypt the most characteristic type of wisdom book was that which is known as the Instruction. The period during which such books were composed was a very long one: the earliest were written well before 2000 B.C. One of the latest of them, the *Instruction of Amen-em-opet*, probably to be dated at some time between 1000 and 600 B.C., served directly as a basis for one section of Proverbs (22: 17 – 24: 22). They usually take the form of advice and warnings given by a father to his son, a feature which is reflected in Proverbs with its frequent use of the phrase 'my son'. One of their most conspicuous features is the predominance of the imperative forms 'Do this', 'Do not do that'. For example, in one of the oldest of them, the *Instruction of the Vizier Ptah-hotep*, the father says to his son, 'Do not become boastful because of your knowledge; do not

3

be over-confident because you are a wise man.' This feature is also frequently found in Proverbs.

The 'father-to-son' form no doubt goes back to a time when education in Egypt was provided by parents; but the Instructions with which we are familiar were mainly used in the school. Egypt had a highly developed system of both elementary and higher education.

It is not difficult to understand how Israel came to borrow this foreign literary tradition. When Israel first became a national state and began to develop settled national institutions, in the time of David and Solomon, it drew upon the experience of other more well-established states such as Egypt. The Egyptian civil servants who helped these Israelite kings to set up their national organizations – including an educational system – were themselves trained in the Egyptian schools, and they brought with them, and handed on, the literary wisdom tradition which had been the basis of their own education. In this way the small group of men who had been selected to occupy the position of state official or scribe in Israel came to found a literary wisdom of their own, closely modelled at first on the Egyptian tradition which they had received. The wisdom tradition in Israel was therefore from the first not a popular tradition but one which was primarily the possession of this privileged, educated class. As we shall see, there were other influences as well, and the Israelite writers did not forget their own distinctive national characteristics; nevertheless Israelite wisdom literature, of which Proverbs is the most characteristic example, took its origin from foreign inspiration.

We cannot be certain that any part of the book goes back to Solomon as is claimed in the headings in 1: 1; 10: 1; 25: 1. But the statement in 1 Kings 4: 32 that Solomon 'uttered three thousand proverbs' is unlikely to be without any historical foundation at all. Prov. 25: 1, with its reference to the work of the 'men of Hezekiah king of Judah' on older proverbial material, shows that the Judaean court was still a centre of wisdom activity 300 years after Solomon, and it is reasonable to suppose that much of Proverbs as we have it now is the product of a continuous development of literary wisdom throughout the period of the monarchy, that is from the tenth to the sixth century B.C.

Egypt was not the only source of influence on Israel's wisdom tradition. The old tribal wisdom of the Israelites can hardly have failed to make its mark upon it, though unfortunately we know very little about this, and are therefore unable to measure the extent of its influence. Another source of influence difficult to assess is that of the Canaanite cities which had existed in Palestine long before the arrival of Israel, and whose higher culture had a marked effect on their new masters when they were conquered or otherwise taken over by David and Solomon when those kings extended Israelite control over the whole country. This Canaanite culture was a mixed one, influenced both by Egypt and the Mesopotamian cultures but also possessing characteristics of its own. Unfortunately the very small quantity of Canaanite wisdom literature which has survived makes it difficult to assess the extent of its influence. Besides these sources, Israel was aware of yet other wisdom traditions: the statement in 1 Kings 4: 30-1 that 'Solomon's wisdom surpassed that of all the men of the east and of all Egypt. For he was wiser than any man, wiser than Ethan the Ezrahite, and Heman, Kalcol, and Darda, the sons of Mahol', and the headings of Prov. 30: 1; 31: 1 (on which see the notes in the commentary) show that there was a wisdom tradition among the tribes east of Palestine, in the northern Arabian desert, with which Israel was in contact.

Far more is known, however, about the influence of Mesopotamian wisdom on Israel. Much of the wisdom literature of the Sumerians and of the Babylonians and Assyrians who followed them in the Euphrates valley has been preserved, although our sources are less abundant than in the case of Egypt. One of the most important characteristics of this wisdom literature is that, unlike that of Egypt where the

Instruction form ('Do this'; 'Do not do that') predominates, much of it takes the form of collections of short proverbs and sayings in which the teaching is expressed partly or wholly in statements which simply describe the facts of life. It is this type rather than the Instruction which predominates also in the greater part of Proverbs. In this respect the *Words of Ahikar*, a book which is probably of Assyrian origin, is particularly important. Much of its contents is very similar to passages in Proverbs: for example, its teaching on parental discipline is very close indeed: 'The son who is educated and disciplined and whose feet are fettered will do well. Do not hesitate to take the rod to your son if you cannot restrain him from wickedness. If I strike you, my son, you will not die, and if I leave you to your own devices you will not live' (lines 80–2). Compare especially Prov. 23: 13–14:

> Do not withhold discipline from a boy;
> take the stick to him, and save him from death.
> If you take the stick to him yourself,
> you will preserve him from the jaws of death.

Similar teaching is also found in Prov. 13: 24; 19: 18; 29: 17.

Ahikar is of particular interest to the student of Proverbs for several reasons. It was almost certainly written in Assyria during the period of the Israelite monarchy, and so is probably contemporary with some parts of Proverbs. It is known to have been composed in scribal circles similar to those of Egypt, and so confirms the view that such circles were the centres of the composition of proverb collections; and finally there is positive proof that it was actually known to, and read by, Israelites: a copy, in Aramaic translation, was found among documents from a Jewish colony in Egypt of the fifth century B.C.

As in the case of Egyptian wisdom literature it is not difficult to understand how this Mesopotamian literature came to exercise its influence on Israel. We know that it was known and read in Canaan even before the arrival of the Israelites,

6

since clay tablets inscribed with proverbs and instructions in Accadian, the language of the Babylonians, have been found in Canaanite cities. This wisdom tradition may therefore have found its way to Israel through the medium of the Canaanites. And in later centuries contacts between Israel and Mesopotamia continued, both in times of peace and in periods when kings of Israel and Judah were the vassals of Assyria and Babylon. At no time was Israel entirely isolated from either Egypt or Mesopotamia.

THE BOOK OF PROVERBS AND ITS MODELS: RESEMBLANCES AND DIFFERENCES

Each area of the ancient Near East developed its own style of wisdom literature, in which local religious and cultural characteristics modified the common pattern. It is therefore important for the student of Proverbs to understand what the book has in common with its models and to what extent it diverges from them.

1. *Scope.* Although at least some sections of Proverbs must have been composed, like their foreign counterparts, mainly for use as textbooks in schools whose purpose was to educate a small scribal class, the tone of the book as a whole is less purely professional than that of the majority of the Egyptian Instructions, and much of its teaching is of more general interest. This may be due to a progressive enlargement of the educated class in Israel during the course of its history. During the later stages of its composition the book tended to lose its purely scholastic character and came to be read by a wider circle of readers for both instruction and entertainment.

2. *Religious teaching.* The Egyptian and Mesopotamian wisdom books are concerned above all to recommend to the student a course of behaviour which will set him on the road to a long, happy and successful career. This was to be achieved, however, not by a selfish careerism but by recognizing that the world is governed by an all-pervading divine Order, and

7

that what is required of a man is simply that he should conform to this Order in every department of life. The man who did so would be happy and prosperous; the man who set himself against the Order would end in disaster. Each man would get what he deserved. This teaching is well summarized in *Ptah-hotep*: 'Truth (that is, the Order) is good and of permanent value, and has remained unchanged since the day when it was created. Whoever breaks its rules is punished. It lies before the uninstructed like a straight path. Wrong-doing has never yet brought its undertakings safe home to port. Evil may indeed acquire wealth, but the strength of truth lies in its permanence, and the righteous man says, "It is an inheritance from my father."'

Basically the teaching of Proverbs follows the same lines. The concept is wide enough to include the practical, moral and religious aspects of life, and in Proverbs, as in its foreign models, these are not sharply distinguished one from the other. The ideals represented by the figures of the wise man and the righteous man are not opposed to one another but are twin aspects of one and the same ideal. Both lead to divine approval and so to happiness.

Nevertheless the unique character of the religion of Israel, though this is hardly ever referred to specifically in Proverbs, left its mark. In the polytheistic systems of Egypt and Meso-potamia there was a multiplicity of gods, none of whom was by himself in supreme control of the universe, and the Order to which men were expected to conform was distinct from and superior to the gods – an impersonal force. But the Israelite's conviction that everything in heaven and earth was under the control of his God, Yahweh (this personal name of God, too sacred to be spoken, is represented in the Old Testament by the phrase 'the LORD'), enabled him, in the end, to see more clearly than his neighbours the true relationship between wisdom and religious faith. This insight is not apparent in every part of Proverbs, but in its final form, which represents the full maturity of Israelite thought on this subject, the book

8

teaches that wisdom is first and foremost the possession of God himself. This insight is most completely expressed in 2: 3–8:

> If you summon discernment to your aid
> and invoke understanding,
> if you seek her out like silver
> and dig for her like buried treasure,
> then you will understand the fear of the LORD
> and attain to the knowledge of God;
> for the LORD bestows wisdom
> and teaches knowledge and understanding.
> Out of his store he endows the upright with ability
> as a shield for those who live blameless lives;
> for he guards the course of justice
> and keeps watch over the way of his loyal servants.

In other passages (1: 20–33; 8; 9: 1–6) the same thought is expressed in vivid symbolism: wisdom is there represented as a personal being related to God, who offers divine instruction to men. This teaching, which provides a counterbalance to the tendency of some strands of Israelite thought to regard wisdom as essentially human arrogance leading to rebellion against God, eventually came to make an important contribution not only to Jewish faith but to Christian teaching as well.

This reconciliation between the originally foreign wisdom tradition and the religion of Israel was not achieved all at once or without a struggle. Wisdom, with its connections with the small ruling class and its tendency to recommend a utilitarian approach to life and in particular to the conduct of national policy, came under fire from some of the prophets, who believed that the only motivation for human conduct ought to be the will of God expressed in the laws which he had given to his people and in the Word which he continued to speak through his prophets. But the decisions of national policy were made on the basis of what the prophets considered to be purely human considerations, such as are expressed in Prov. 11: 14:

For want of skilful strategy an army is lost;
victory is the fruit of long planning.

For the prophets, victory was secured not by skilful strategy but by hearing and obeying the Word of God. And so we find the prophet Isaiah condemning human wisdom:

Then the LORD said:

Because this people approach me with their mouths
    and honour me with their lips
  while their hearts are far from me,
and their religion is but a precept of men, learnt by rote,
therefore I will yet again shock this people,
  adding shock to shock:
  the wisdom of their wise men shall vanish
  and the discernment of the discerning shall be lost.

(Isa. 29: 13–14)

It was probably from this time onwards that attempts were first made to reconcile the wisdom tradition with the will of God. Isaiah himself showed the way: he was the first, as far as we know, to use the word 'wise' of God when he affirmed that God's control of history was inspired by wisdom (Isa. 31: 2). But the later years of the monarchy were not, on the whole, years when the prophets found a ready ear in court circles. In the seventh century B.C. Jeremiah continued to attack the policies of the kings of his time, and it was almost certainly not until the period after the destruction of the state of Judah in 587 B.C., when men were able to reflect on the experiences of the past with some degree of theological perspective, that the final reconciliation between the 'fear of Yahweh' and wisdom was achieved.

Proverbs therefore reflects a series of stages in the development of Israel's own brand of wisdom teaching: it contains Instructions hardly distinguishable from those of Egypt, many sayings in which, in spite of an Israelite dress, the successful life remains the goal with little reference to specifically moral or religious considerations, and finally – particularly in parts of chapters 1–9 – passages in which the overriding consideration is the pursuit of a wisdom which is in entire conformity with the 'fear of the LORD'. In the commentary an attempt will be made to distinguish these various stages.

3. *Universality.* There is one respect in which Proverbs, like the other wisdom books of the Old Testament, has completely preserved the character of the international wisdom tradition. This is its complete silence about national concerns. Apart from the references in some of the section headings to Solomon and Hezekiah and the frequent references to Yahweh ('the LORD'), the God of Israel, there is nothing to make the reader aware that this is part of the literature of Israel. This remarkable fact marks out the wisdom books of the Old Testament and puts them in a class by themselves. Elsewhere in the Old Testament there is hardly a page where there is not some reference to Israel, its history, its special relationship with Yahweh, its sense of being guided by him and of obligation to him and its rejection of all other gods. In Proverbs there is nothing of this. God is frequently mentioned as the ruler of the universe and the arbiter of man's destiny, and is known by his name, Yahweh; but the other characteristics of God familiar to us from the other parts of the Old Testament such as his love, holiness, jealousy and election of Israel as his own people are entirely absent. Proverbs, like its foreign counterparts, appears to be addressed not to a particular nation but to the individual, whoever he may be. Its observations and advice are applicable to anyone. This is one of the great merits of the book: whereas elsewhere in the Old Testament the emphasis is on the people of God and the worshipping community, Proverbs takes account of man's individual life and its problems, calling him away *as an individual* from folly and evil and urging him to embrace wisdom and righteousness.

THE STRUCTURE OF THE BOOK

The book consists of at least eight sections, each of which was probably originally a separate work. All of these except one are provided with their own headings (that is, headings in the text itself as distinct from those added by the N.E.B. translators). Each of these will be introduced in its proper place in the commentary.

  1. 1: 1–9: 18. Heading: 'The proverbs of Solomon son of David, king of Israel.'

  2. 10: 1–22: 16. Heading: 'The proverbs of Solomon.'

  3. 22: 17–24: 22. Heading: 'The sayings of the wise.'

  4. 24: 23–34. Heading: 'More sayings of wise men.'

  5. 25–29. Heading: 'More proverbs of Solomon transcribed by the men of Hezekiah king of Judah.'

  6. 30: 1–33. Heading: 'Sayings of Agur son of Jakeh from Massa.'

  7. 31: 1–9. Heading: 'Sayings of Lemuel king of Massa, which his mother taught him.'

  8. 31: 10–31. No heading. A poem about the capable wife.

HOW TO READ THE BOOK

  1. The literary forms in which the teaching is expressed are unfamiliar to modern readers. There is little to be gained from attempting to read the book straight through without a break. Close attention should be paid to what is said in the commentary about particular forms, so that each section or sub-section can be studied as an entity. In those parts of the book which consist of long series of mainly unconnected short sayings, each one must be read and savoured individually. The teaching of these sections, including the tensions which sometimes exist between one saying and another, will emerge most clearly if the sayings are grouped together under thematic headings, such as wealth and poverty, laziness and diligence, education, speech and silence, etc. The *List of Subjects* on pp.

187–9 is given as an example of such a classification. The reader can complete it for himself.

2. Use your imagination and sense of humour. Statements like 'A door turns on its hinges, a sluggard on his bed' (26: 14) are intended to be amusing, and to treat them solemnly would be to miss the point. A little imagination used to visualize the situations lying behind many of the sayings will reveal a vivid picture of a real human society in all its variety. The book has been compared to Balzac's *Comédie humaine*, a series of novels which portrays nineteenth-century French society in all its complexity, from the highest social class to the lowest. A comparison with the novels of Dickens would be equally appropriate. For a host of characters pass through its pages: the farmer, the courtier, the drop-out, the dishonest trader, the adulterous woman, the husband absent on business, the street gang, the schoolboy and the teacher, the rather simple young man, the prostitute, the thief, the gossip, the royal messenger, and many more.

3. What of its religious value? The place of Proverbs in the religious development of Israel has already been sketched. There is no disguising the fact that on the moral level there are wide differences, ranging from the recommendation to love one's enemies in 25: 21–2, which Paul quoted in Rom. 12: 20, to sayings which appear to encourage self-interest, not to say sharp practice. Clearly Proverbs cannot be used in its entirety either as a moral handbook or as a guide to spirituality. It lacks the passion and the moral earnestness of the prophets. But it shows us a people wrestling with a problem which faces us all today: how to live and work in the world and keep one's feet firmly on the ground while at the same time acknowledging the claims of God and trusting in his guidance of the world. Like the other books of the Old Testament it is in one sense a very human book; but it is also rooted in a confident religious faith.

✲ ✲ ✲ ✲ ✲ ✲ ✲ ✲ ✲ ✲ ✲ ✲ ✲

SECTION I. PROVERBS 1-9

Chapters 1–9 (the N.E.B. divides this section into two – chapters 1–7 and 8–9) in their present form teach a concept of wisdom which is the most fully developed of any in the book: wisdom is not only a practical guide to the successful life but a characteristic of God himself, from whom alone it can be obtained. This theological interpretation of wisdom marks this section out as the latest in date. It was placed at the beginning of the book by the final editor to set the tone of the whole and to indicate the way in which the subsequent sections were to be understood.

But these chapters are themselves the result of a long and complex process of composition. The original kernel was a book rather similar to the Egyptian Instructions (see pp. 3–4) and consisted of a general introduction followed by a series of ten short chapters or Instructions in which a wisdom teacher laid down those basic principles of conduct which, if followed consistently, were a sure guide to a happy and successful life. In this original book the word 'wisdom' did not play a key role, and there was no suggestion that it was a characteristic of God.

To this kernel various kinds of supplementary material came to be added, of which two groups are especially important since their purpose was to reinterpret the original work and to present its teaching in a new light. In the first of these groups the idea of 'wisdom' is taken as a basic concept and equated with the words of the teacher. In some of these passages wisdom is represented as an object of infinite value to be obtained at all costs; in others it is personified and portrayed as a female figure, sometimes as a teacher and sometimes as a bride, who offers the secret of life to any young man who will accept her invitation. At this stage there was still no suggestion that this Wisdom was associated with God. That was a further development which was made by the second group of additional passages which represent

Wisdom as an inseparable attribute of God himself. In the commentary an attempt is made to distinguish these three strands.

Advice to the reader

THE PROLOGUE

THE PROVERBS of Solomon son of David, king of **1**
    Israel,
by which men will come to wisdom and instruction   2
and will understand words that bring understanding,
and by which they will gain a well-instructed 3
    intelligence,
righteousness, justice, and probity.
The simple will be endowed with shrewdness   4
and the young with knowledge and prudence.
If the wise man listens, he will increase his learning,   5
and the man of understanding will acquire skill
to understand proverbs and parables,   6
the sayings of wise men and their riddles.

The fear of the LORD is the beginning*a* of knowledge, 7
but fools scorn wisdom and discipline.

✶ Verses 1–5 closely resemble the prologue to the Egyptian *Instruction of Amen-em-opet*, and originally formed an introduction to the book of ten Instructions, in which the author commended his book to the reader. Now, together with verses 6–7, they form the introduction to the whole book of Proverbs.

1. *The proverbs of Solomon*: the attribution of wisdom books to kings was a regular practice in the ancient Near East. Here

[a] *Or* chief part.

it is an acknowledgment of Solomon's contribution to the wisdom movement in Israel.

3. *righteousness, justice, and probity*: these qualities, as well as such less obviously moral qualities as *shrewdness* and *prudence* (verse 4), were frequently stressed in the wisdom books of the ancient Near East, although the specific mention of them here in the introduction to the book possibly indicates an increased emphasis on them which may be due to Israelite religious influence.

6. *riddles*: the asking and answering of riddles was a form of entertainment which also had its serious side. Solomon's reputation for wisdom depended partly on his ability to answer riddles ('hard questions' in 1 Kings 10: 1 is the same word in Hebrew as *riddles* here); and in the stories of Samson (Judg. 14: 5–20) we see how serious a matter riddling could be. The sayings in Prov. 30: 15–31 may be based on riddles.

7. This verse, which implies that human *knowledge* is obtainable only by those who possess God's blessing, belongs to the final strand of material in these chapters. *The fear of the LORD* means obedience to the will of God made known through the religion of Israel. ✳

AVOID BAD COMPANY (1)

8 Attend, my son, to your father's instruction
    and do not reject the teaching of your mother;
9 for they are a garland of grace on your head
    and a chain of honour round your neck.

10,11 My son, bad men may tempt you[a] and say,
      'Come with us; let us lie in wait for someone's blood;
      let us waylay[b] an innocent man who has done us no
        harm.
12   Like Sheol we will swallow them alive;

[a] Prob. rdg.; Heb. adds do not come, or, with some MSS., do not consent.   [b] Prob. rdg.; Heb. store up.

16

> though blameless, they shall be like men who go down
>   to the abyss.
>
> We shall take rich treasure of every sort   13
> and fill our homes with booty;
> throw in your lot with us,   14
> and we will have a common purse.'
>
> My son, do not go along with them,   15
> keep clear of their ways;
> they hasten hot-foot into crime,   16
>   impatient to shed blood.
>
> In vain is a net spread wide   17
> if any bird that flies can see it.
>
> These men lie in wait for their own blood   18
> and waylay[a] no one but themselves.
> This is the fate[b] of men eager for ill-gotten gain: 19
> it robs those who get it of their lives.

✻ This is THE FIRST OF THE ORIGINAL INSTRUCTIONS. No additions have been made to it. The theme is an appropriate one for the education of young men, and occurs in other ancient Near Eastern wisdom books.

8–9. The introduction, in which the teacher stresses the importance of his words and urges the pupil to pay attention to them, is characteristic of the Instruction form and occurs at the beginning of each of the Instructions in this section.

8. *Attend*: literally, 'hear'. This is a key word in the Egyptian Instructions.

my son: for this expression see p. 3. The reference here and in some other passages in Proverbs to the *mother* is not regularly found in non-Israelite wisdom books, and raises the question whether in Israel these Instructions may have been used in the home as well as in the school.

[a] *Prob. rdg.; Heb.* store up.
[b] This...fate: *prob. rdg.; Heb.* Such are the courses.

9. *garland of grace*: the word *grace* has no theological sense here but merely means 'attractiveness'.

12. *Sheol* in the Old Testament is the place to which men go when they die. The thought that Sheol *swallows* its victims *alive* was probably derived from a mythological belief that death was a god into whose mouth the dead descended.

17. This is a difficult verse. If the N.E.B. translation is correct, the teacher is warning his pupil not to be stupid like his would-be companions, who are blind to the inevitable fate which will follow their misdeeds, and so more foolish even than the birds, who avoid an obvious trap.

18–19. There is nothing miraculous about the fate of these ruffians: the meaning is simply that they will eventually be caught and executed for their crimes. But the certainty with which this is predicted is based on the common ancient Near Eastern belief that those who oppose the Order of the universe (see pp. 7–8) will inevitably suffer. ✳

WISDOM OFFERS HER ADVICE

20 Wisdom cries aloud in the open air,
  she raises her voice in public places;
21 she calls at the top of the busy street
  and proclaims at the open gates of the city:
22 'Simple fools, how long will you be content with your
    simplicity?[a]
23 If only you would respond to my reproof,
  I would give you my counsel
  and teach you my precepts.
24 But because you refused to listen when I called,
  because no one attended when I stretched out my hand,
25 because you spurned all my advice
  and would have nothing to do with my reproof,
26 I in my turn will laugh at your doom

[a] *The rest of verse 22 transposed to follow verse 27.*

and deride you when terror comes upon you,
when terror comes upon you like a hurricane   27
and your doom descends like a whirlwind.[a]
Insolent men delight in their insolence;
stupid men hate knowledge.[b]
When they call upon me, I will not answer them;   28
when they search for me, they shall not find me.
Because they hate knowledge   29
and have not chosen to fear the LORD,
because they have not accepted my counsel   30
and have spurned all my reproof,
they shall eat the fruits of their behaviour   31
and have a surfeit of their own devices;
for the simpleton turns a deaf ear and comes to grief,   32
and the stupid are ruined by their own complacency.
But whoever listens to me shall live without a care,   33
undisturbed by fear of misfortune.'

* In this passage Wisdom is represented as a woman teacher
who stands in a busy part of the city addressing the crowd and
urging them to stop and listen to her teaching. (The word for
'wisdom' in Hebrew is feminine.) The claim which she makes
(verse 33) is similar to that made by the human teachers in
the Instructions. This personification of Wisdom is peculiar to
Israelite wisdom literature, and many attempts have been made
to explain it. Further personifications of Wisdom are found in
8: 1–36 and 9: 1–6. In this case it is probably no more than a
vivid way of presenting the teaching of the Instructions: instead of the schoolmaster, it is the teaching itself which comes
to life and pleads with the pupil to pay attention !
Apart from the isolated reference to God in verse 29
Wisdom is the central figure, and the passage belongs to the

[a] *Prob. rdg.; Heb. adds* when anguish and distress come upon you.
[b] Insolent...knowledge: *transposed from end of verse 22.*

first group of additions to the original book of Instructions: Wisdom is nowhere associated with God. The passage makes perfectly good sense without verse 29, which belongs to the second group of additions in which Wisdom is made dependent on the *fear* of *the LORD*.

21. The *gates of the city* were the place where the business of the city, administrative, legal and commercial, was transacted. This open-air appeal of Wisdom has been compared with that of the prophets, and her words have some similarity to the prophetic appeal for repentance. It has also been suggested that the wisdom teachers may have stood in the streets appealing for clients, though there is no evidence for this view. But anyone who had news to communicate or wares to sell would probably have done so.

22. *Simple fools*: the Hebrew word is regularly used in the wisdom literature to denote the young man whose character is as yet unformed by education, and who is open to persuasion, good or bad, as distinct from the *insolent men* and the *stupid men* (verse 27) who are beyond all hope of rehabilitation.

30–2. Here again we find the belief that disobedience to the Order, of which the wisdom teacher and his teaching are a part, brings inevitable retribution. ✻

AVOID THE ADULTERESS (I)

2 My son, if you take my words to heart
  and lay up my commands in your mind,

2   giving your attention to wisdom
  and your mind to understanding,

3   if you summon discernment to your aid
  and invoke understanding,

4   if you seek her out like silver
  and dig for her like buried treasure,

5   then you will understand the fear of the LORD
  and attain to the knowledge of God;

for the LORD bestows wisdom   6
and teaches knowledge and understanding.
Out of his store he endows the upright with ability   7
as a shield for those who live blameless lives;
for he guards the course of justice   8
and keeps watch over the way of his loyal servants.

Then you will understand what is right and just   9
and keep*a* only to the good man's path;
for wisdom will sink into your mind,   10
and knowledge will be your heart's delight.
Prudence will keep watch over you,   11
understanding will guard you,
it will save you from evil ways   12
and from men whose talk is subversive,
who forsake the honest course   13
to walk in ways of darkness,
who rejoice in doing evil   14
and exult in evil and subversive acts,
whose own ways are crooked,   15
whose tracks are devious.
It will save you from the adulteress,*b*   16
from the loose woman*c* with her seductive words,
who forsakes the teaching of her childhood   17
and has forgotten the covenant of her God;
for her path*d* runs downhill towards death,   18
and her course is set for the land of the dead.
No one who resorts to her*e* finds his way back   19
or regains the path to life.

[a] keep: *prob. rdg.; Heb.* uprightness.
[b] *Lit.* strange woman.
[c] *Lit.* alien woman.
[d] *Prob. rdg.; Heb.* house.
[e] resorts to her: *or* takes to them.

20 See then that you follow the footsteps of good men
     and keep to the course of the righteous;
21 for the upright shall dwell on earth
     and blameless men remain there;
22 but the wicked shall be uprooted from it
     and traitors weeded out.

* Hidden within this chapter is the SECOND OF THE INSTRUC-
TIONS; it has been overlaid with much additional material, and
the result is a long, rather vague and repetitious discourse, in
which the only definite instruction occurs in verses 16–19.
It is these verses which constituted the original Instruction,
together with its original introduction, verses 1 and 9. (*It
will save you* in verse 16, which originally followed verse 9,
could equally well be translated '*This* will save you'.) The
original introduction has been expanded in two stages: verses
2–4 identify the teacher's words with an infinitely precious
commodity called 'wisdom' which can only be found after
careful search. In verses 5–8 comes the final stage in the development of the thought: wisdom is now seen as the gift
of God.

Verses 10–15 belong to the same stage as verses 2–4: they
expand the *what is right and just* of verse 9 in terms of wisdom,
but without reference to God. The last verses (20–2) are very
general in character, and are unlikely to have belonged to the
original Instruction, which ends dramatically in verse 19.

5. *the fear of the LORD*: see the note on 1: 7.

16–19. Warnings against sexual immorality are characteristic of this section: compare 5: 3–23; 6: 24–35; 7: 4–27. As in
similar passages in the non-Israelite wisdom literature, the
author of these passages probably intended his warnings to be
taken literally. But elsewhere in the Old Testament adultery
is used as a symbol for Israel's unfaithfulness to God; and the
editor of this section of the book may have had this idea in
mind: after the appeal by Wisdom in 1: 20–33 it is natural to

22

think of the adulteress as Wisdom's opposite – that is, as a symbol of the 'unwisdom' of abandoning the 'fear of the LORD' in favour of the worship of other gods.

16. The use of rather unusual Hebrew words for *adulteress* and *loose woman* has led some commentators to suppose that the woman referred to here is a foreigner (see the N.E.B. footnotes); but more probably the meaning in each case is 'wife of another man', i.e. an adulteress.

17. *teaching*: another possible rendering is 'companion': that is, the woman has deserted the husband whom she married in her youth. In that case the *covenant of her God* would be the marriage relationship, sanctified by divine protection and approval. If adultery here is interpreted symbolically as religious unfaithfulness the phrase acquires the further meaning of Israel's relationship to God.

18. *death*: this is not necessarily an exaggeration: Lev. 20: 10 prescribes the death penalty for such a case. Elsewhere in Proverbs (5: 9–14) the penalty foreseen is exclusion from the community, which might well result in the death of the offender, who would now be without protection.

the land of the dead: compare the Babylonian phrase 'the land of no return'. The reference is to a subterranean kingdom ruled by Death: compare 1: 12. The *path* along which the adulteress leads the young man to her house is dramatically identified with that which leads to the land of the dead; compare 7: 25–7.

21. *dwell on earth*: this phrase could also mean 'dwell in the land'. In that case the reference would be to God's promise of the land of Canaan to Israel. ✳

TRUST AND HONOUR GOD

My son, do not forget my teaching,　　　　　　　　　　**3**
　　but guard my commands in your heart;
　for long life and years in plenty　　　　　　　　　　2
　　will they bring you, and prosperity as well.

3 Let your good faith and loyalty never fail,
   but bind them about your neck.[a]

4 Thus will you win favour and success
   in the sight of God and man.

5 Put all your trust in the LORD
   and do not rely on your own understanding.

6 Think of him in all your ways,
   and he will smooth your path.

7 Do not think how wise you are,
   but fear the LORD and turn from evil.

8 Let that be the medicine to keep you in health,
   the liniment for your limbs.

9 Honour the LORD with your wealth
   as the first charge on all your earnings;

10 then your granaries will be filled with corn[b]
   and your vats bursting with new wine.

11 My son, do not spurn the LORD's correction
   or take offence at his reproof;

12 for those whom he loves the LORD reproves,
   and he punishes a favourite son.

✶ This THIRD INSTRUCTION consists of a series of warnings about proper behaviour towards God, preceded by an introduction (verses 1–4) similar to 1: 8–9. The behaviour recommended – reliance on God, humility, due performance of sacrificial duties and acceptance of divine reproof – is of a very general kind, although some of the phraseology suggests that Israelite religious influence may have left its mark.

1–4. The terms in which the high value of the teacher's words is expressed are reminiscent of Egyptian Instructions, especially *Amen-em-opet*, although there is some similarity to expressions found elsewhere in the Old Testament.

[a] *So Sept.; Heb. adds* and write them on the tablet of your mind.
[b] with corn: *or* to overflowing.

1. *guard my commands in your heart*: compare *Amen-em-opet*
3: 11, 'it is good to put them in your heart', but also Jer. 31: 33,
'I will set my law within them and write it on their hearts.'

2. *long life...and prosperity*: compare *Amen-em-opet* 4: 1–2:

> You will find my words a storehouse of life,
> and your body will prosper on earth.

3. *bind them about your neck*: compare Deut. 6: 8: 'Bind
them as a sign on the hand.'

9. *Honour the LORD with your wealth*: this means offering
part of one's crop to God as a sacrifice in recognition that it
was he who gave it. Such an offering of firstfruits is prescribed
in Exod. 23: 19 and other Old Testament laws, although there
is nothing specifically Israelite about such a piece of advice: in
the Egyptian *Wisdom of Ani*, for example, we read, 'Celebrate
the festival of your god...God is angry with those who
neglect him...To receive reverence is his right. The god will
exalt the name of him who does this.' This is the only passage
in Proverbs where sacrifice is specifically commanded. Like
their foreign counterparts, the authors of Proverbs recognized
its desirability but, as wisdom teachers, did not make it one of
their chief concerns.

11–12. These verses recognize the possibility that even
those who serve and honour God sometimes meet with
misfortune, and seek to give an explanation of this. Such
troubles are God's way of disciplining *those whom he loves*:
they are a proof of his favour. Compare Job 5: 17, and also the
late Egyptian Instruction known as *Papyrus Insinger* (XVII
20: 13): 'Recognize the hand of God in misfortune when it
comes upon you.' These two verses are quoted in the Epistle
to the Hebrews (12: 5–6), where – in the succeeding verses –
great emphasis is laid on the significance of the word *son*: the
fact that the Christians are enduring suffering shows that they
are truly the sons of their heavenly Father.   *

THE INFINITE VALUE OF WISDOM

13 Happy he who has found wisdom,
and the man who has acquired understanding;
14 for wisdom is more profitable than silver,
and the gain she brings is better than gold.
15 She is more precious than red coral,
and all your jewels are no match for her.
16 Long life is in her right hand,
in her left hand are riches and honour.
17 Her ways are pleasant ways
and all her paths lead to prosperity.
18 She is a staff of life to all who grasp her,
and those who hold her fast are safe.

19 In wisdom the LORD founded the earth
and by understanding he set the heavens in their place;
20 by his knowledge the depths burst forth
and the clouds dropped dew.

* The fact that these verses are not addressed to the pupil but
are a general statement shows that they are unconnected with
the passage which precedes them. In fact there are two poems
here, corresponding to the two groups of additional material
referred to on pp. 14–15.

13–18. In this poem the long life and prosperity which the
wisdom teacher promises elsewhere as the consequence of
following his instruction (e.g. in 3: 1–4) are claimed as the
consequence of the possession of an infinitely precious 'wisdom'. There is more than a suggestion of personification here:
it is not quite clear whether wisdom is an object of great
value as in 2: 4, or a woman. Here wisdom is not associated
with God: this poem belongs to the first group of additional
material.

16. It has been suggested that the imagery in this verse may

26

have been derived from the way in which the Egyptian goddess Maat, the goddess of Truth and Order, is represented pictorially as holding in her hands objects which symbolize *long life* and *riches and honour.*

19–20. In this second poem, which belongs to the second group of additional material, a further theological step is taken: the author asserts that wisdom has been God's possession from the very beginning, since it was *In* (or, 'by') *wisdom* that he *founded the earth.*

The description of the creation of the world in these verses follows a common tradition. The earth, conceived of as a flat disc, was first *founded*, that is, settled on foundations or pillars which reached down into the subterranean ocean; next the solid hemispherical dome of the heavens (the 'vault' of Gen. 1: 6) was placed over it, and finally the earth was watered by the provision of holes or trapdoors in the earth's surface, through which the springs bubbled up, and in the heavens, for the rain and *dew.* See *Old Testament Illustrations*, p. 26. ✳

BE KIND AND GENEROUS TO OTHERS

My son, keep watch over your ability and prudence,	21
do not let them slip from sight;	
they shall be a charm*a* hung about your neck	22
and an ornament on your breast.*b*	
Then you will go your way without a care,	23
and your feet will not stumble.	
When you sit,*c* you need have no fear;	24
when you lie down, your sleep will be pleasant.	
Do not be afraid when fools are frightened	25
or when ruin comes upon the wicked;	
for the LORD will be at your side,	26
and he will keep your feet clear of the trap.	

[a] charm: *lit.* life.   [b] breast: *lit.* throat.
[c] *So Sept.; Heb.* lie down.

27 Refuse no man any favour that you owe him
    when it lies in your power to pay it.

28 Do not say to your friend, 'Come back again;
    you shall have it tomorrow'—when you have it already.

29 Plot no evil against your friend,
    your unsuspecting neighbour.

30 Do not pick a quarrel with a man for no reason,
    if he has not done you a bad turn.

31 Do not emulate a lawless man,
    do not choose to follow his footsteps;

32 for one who is not straight is detestable to the LORD,
    but upright men are in God's confidence.

33 The LORD's curse rests on the house of the evildoer,
    while he blesses the home of the righteous.

34 Though God himself meets the arrogant with
     arrogance,
    yet he bestows his favour on the meek.*

35 Wise men are adorned with* honour,
    but the coat* on a fool's back is contempt.

✷ Originally this FOURTH INSTRUCTION consisted of verses
27–31, preceded by an introduction (verses 21–4) and possibly
followed by a conclusion in verses 34–5. The central section
(verses 27–31) consists of a series of short warnings about
kindliness and neighbourliness. The introduction has been
expanded by the addition of verses 25–6, which assert that the
protection from fear and harm promised by the teacher is
really provided by God; there is a similar addition in
verses 32–3. The earlier stage, in which the teacher's words
were identified with wisdom but without any association with
God, is not represented here.

[a] *Or* wretched.
[b] are adorned with: *prob. rdg.; Heb.* shall inherit.
[c] the coat: *prob. rdg.; Heb. obscure.*

21–2. The introduction differs from the introduction to the other Instructions (e.g. 1: 8; 3: 1–2) in that it refers not to the teacher's words but to *your ability and prudence*. The Septuagint (the principal ancient Greek translation) has probably preserved the original text: 'Guard *my* counsel.'

a charm hung about your neck: an alternative translation would be 'life for your soul', that is, 'your source of vitality'.

23–6. The idea of life as a journey from the dangers of which wisdom (or God) will protect the traveller is a frequent one in Proverbs.

31. The theme of this verse is the same as that of 1: 10–19.

32. *detestable to the LORD*: this phrase occurs also in Deuteronomy. But a similar phrase is frequently used in *Amen-em-opet*, and there is not necessarily a connection with the Old Testament religious tradition here.

35. The second line of this verse is based on an emendation of a Hebrew text whose meaning is not clear (see the N.E.B. footnote). ✳

THE VALUE OF TRADITIONAL WISDOM

Listen, my sons, to a father's instruction,   **4**
  consider attentively how to gain understanding;
for it is sound learning I give you;   2
  so do not forsake my teaching.
I too have been a father's son,   3
  tender in years, my mother's only child.
He taught me and said to me: 4
Hold fast to my words with all your heart,
keep my commands and you will have life.
*a*Do not forget or turn a deaf ear to what I say.   5

The first thing*b* is to acquire wisdom;   7
  gain understanding though it cost you all you have.

[a] *So Sept.; Heb. prefixes* Get wisdom, get understanding.
[b] *Prob. rdg.; Heb. adds* wisdom.

6 Do not forsake her, and she will keep you safe;
 love her, and she will guard you;
8 cherish her, and she will lift you high;
 if only you embrace her, she will bring you to honour.
9 She will set a garland of grace on your head
 and bestow on you a crown of glory.

* The FIFTH INSTRUCTION, preserved in verses 1–5, seems originally to have been simply an appeal to take the teacher's instruction seriously. But in the other Instructions this appeal is confined to the introduction. It is possible that what we have here is an expanded introduction to an Instruction of which the main section has disappeared. However this may be, verses 6–9 have been added in order to identify the words of the teacher with wisdom: compare *do not forsake my teaching* (verse 2) with *Do not forsake her* (verse 6). (The N.E.B. has reversed the order of verses 6 and 7 in order to make better sense of a difficult text.) The final stage, associating wisdom with God, is not represented here.

This passage has close parallels with Egyptian literature. In the *Kemit*, an early book of instruction for Egyptian teachers, we read: 'My father also trained me in the useful writings which had come down to him. Then I found that men praised me, since I had become wise, since my eyes had been opened.' In both cases great stress is laid on the traditional character of the teaching.

5–7. There is considerable confusion in the text here, perhaps caused when verses 6–9 were added. The N.E.B. translation is partly based on the Septuagint and is one of several possible ways of trying to solve the problem.

6–9. Here wisdom is represented as a female figure, though of a different kind from that in 1: 20–33. The metaphor is that of choosing a wife, and verse 9 refers to the wedding, when it was the custom for the bride to place a *garland* or *crown* on the head of the bridegroom. The representation of Wisdom

as a virtuous wife is probably intended in part as a corollary to
the warnings against the adulteress in 2: 16–19 and other
passages. See also the note on 31: 30. ✻

AVOID BAD COMPANY (2)

Listen, my son, take my words to heart,	10
and the years of your life shall be multiplied.	
I will guide you in the paths of wisdom	11
and lead you in honest ways.	
As you walk you will not slip,	12
and, if you run, nothing will bring you down.	
Cling to instruction and never let it go;	13
observe it well, for it is your life.	
Do not take to the course of the wicked	14
or follow the way of evil men;	
do not set foot on it, but avoid it;	15
turn aside and go on your way.	
For they cannot sleep unless they have done some	16
wrong;	
unless they have been someone's downfall they lose	
their sleep.	
The bread they eat is the fruit of crime	17
and they drink wine got by violence.	
The course of the righteous is like morning light,	18
growing brighter till it is broad day;	
but the ways of the wicked are like darkness at night,	19
and they do not know what has been their downfall.	

✻ The theme of this SIXTH INSTRUCTION is similar to that of
1: 10–19. Verses 10–12 form the introduction; verse 13 seems
to be an addition identifying the teaching with wisdom, although instead of 'wisdom' we have one of its synonyms,
'instruction'. The theme of the path of life, which already

occurs in the introduction, is taken up and elaborated in the main section (verses 14–19) in the form of the 'doctrine of the two ways': the ways of the righteous and of the wicked, which lead respectively to a safe destination and to destruction. This ancient theme, which already appears in embryo in one of the earliest Egyptian Instructions, *Ptah-hotep*, continued to be a favourite way of expressing moral teaching in both Judaism and Christianity, and is used in the Sermon on the Mount (Matt. 7: 13–14). ✻

WATCH YOUR STEP

20 My son, attend to my speech,
   pay heed to my words;
21 do not let them slip out of your mind,
   keep them close in your heart;
22 for they are life to him who finds them,
   and health to his whole body.
23 Guard your heart more than any treasure,
   for it is the source of all life.
24 Keep your mouth from crooked speech
   and your lips from deceitful talk.
25 Let your eyes look straight before you,
   fix your gaze upon what lies ahead.
26 Look out for the path that your feet must take,
   and your ways will be secure.
27 Swerve neither to right nor left,
   and keep clear of every evil thing.

✻ In this SEVENTH INSTRUCTION the introduction (verses 20–2) ends with the word *body*, which provides a starting point for the key words *heart, mouth, eyes, feet* which are the pegs on which the Instruction is hung. This kind of schematization is frequent both in the Old Testament and in Near Eastern literature: compare, for example, Ps. 115: 5–7. The teaching is of a very general character, and there are some parallels in the Old Testament, notably in Deuteronomy (e.g. Deut. 28: 14, 'You shall turn neither to the right nor to the left from all the things which I command you this day'); but the parallels with non-Israelite literature are closer. The necessity for keeping a careful watch over one's tongue and over one's behaviour generally was a constant theme of the Egyptian Instructions (and to some extent of the Mesopotamian ones), since they were mainly intended for apprentice courtiers for whom discretion was an essential qualification.

23. *Guard your heart*: in ancient Near Eastern thought the meaning of *heart* was somewhat different from the modern conception of it. We tend to think of it as the seat of the emotions: for example, 'to be ruled by one's heart rather than one's head' means to be governed by one's feelings rather than by one's intelligence. In Near Eastern (and Israelite) thought, however, the heart was the equivalent of what *we* call the head! *Guard your heart* means 'be ruled at all times by your intelligence rather than by your emotions'. Since the heart was thought to be the seat of the intelligence and also of the will, the control of it was more important than anything else.

24. *Keep your mouth*: this verse has very close parallels in Near Eastern wisdom literature, e.g. 'Let your mouth be controlled and your speech guarded' (the Babylonian *Counsels of Wisdom*, line 26); 'Guard your mouth more carefully than anything else' (*Ahikar*, line 98; note that the *form* of this line corresponds very closely to verse 23). The theme is taken up and developed in Jas. 3: 3-12.

25. The guardianship of the *eyes*, that is, not allowing one's eyes to wander or to linger on things which might lead one into temptation, is still a commonplace of Christian moral theology. It is frequently found in non-Israelite wisdom literature and also in the Old Testament, e.g. Ps. 119: 37, 'Turn away my eyes from all that is vile.' ✳

33

AVOID THE ADULTERESS (2)

5   My son, attend to my wisdom
    and listen to my good counsel,

2   so that you may observe proper prudence
    and your speech be informed with knowledge.

3   For though the lips of an adulteress drip honey
    and her tongue is smoother than oil,

4   yet in the end she is more bitter than wormwood,
    and sharp as a two-edged sword.

5   Her feet go downwards on the path to death,
    her course is set for Sheol.

6   She does not watch for the road that leads to life;
    her course turns this way and that, and what does she
        care?[a]

7   Now, my son,[b] listen to me
    and do not ignore what I say:

8   keep well away from her
    and do not go near the door of her house;

9   or you will lose your dignity in the eyes of others
    and your honour before strangers;[c]

10 strangers will batten on your wealth,
    and your hard-won gains pass to another man's
        family.

11 The end will be that you will starve,
    you will shrink to mere skin and bones.

12 Then you will say, 'Why did I hate correction
    and set my heart against reproof?

13 I did not listen to the voice of my teachers
    or pay attention to my masters.

[a] what...care?: *or* she is restless.
[b] my son: *so Sept.; Heb.* O sons.
[c] *Prob. rdg., cp. Targ.; Heb.* before a cruel one.

34

I soon earned*a* a bad name   14
and was despised in the public assembly.'
Drink water from your own cistern   15
and running water from your own spring;
do not let your*b* well overflow into the road,   16
your runnels of water pour into the street;
let them be yours alone,   17
not shared with strangers.
Let your fountain, the wife of your youth,   18
be blessed, rejoice in her,
a lovely doe, a graceful hind, let her be your companion;*c* 19
you will at all times be bathed in her love,
and her love will continually wrap you round.
Wherever you turn, she will guide you;
when you lie in bed, she will watch over you,
and when you wake she will talk with you.*d*
Why, my son, are you wrapped up in the love of an 20
     adulteress?
Why do you embrace a loose woman?
For a man's ways are always in the LORD's sight   21
who watches for every path that he must take.
The wicked man is caught in his own iniquities   22
and held fast in the toils of his own sin;
he will perish for want of discipline,   23
wrapped in the shroud of his boundless folly.

✻ This EIGHTH INSTRUCTION is the second of those concerned
with the avoidance of adultery. Verses 1–2 form the introduction, and the main section consists of verses 3–8, which closely
resemble the other Instructions on the same theme: 2: 16–19;

[a] *Or* I almost earned.
[b] do not let your: *prob. rdg.; Heb.* shall your.
[c] let...companion: *so Sept.; Heb. om.*
[d] Wherever...with you: *transposed from ch. 6 (verse 22).*

6: 24–5; 7: 25–7. Each of the others, however, begins with an introductory phrase about saving the pupil from the designs of scheming women with their seductive words (2: 16; 6: 24; 7: 5). In the Hebrew these phrases resemble one another very closely; and it is probable that the same pattern was originally followed here also: some equivalent phrase has accidentally dropped out between verses 2 and 3. The rest of the chapter also consists of warnings against adultery, but these are of a somewhat different character: more precise and down to earth, and addressed, it would appear, to older married men, whereas the school pupil was presumably unmarried. They must be regarded as later additions. It is not certain what was the original conclusion of this Instruction.

3–8. A sharp contrast is drawn between the delectable promises held out by the adulteress and the terrible fate which befalls those who listen to her.

5. *Sheol*: see the note on 1: 12. The thought is the same as in 2: 18–19.

7. *my son*: in this case the phrase does not mark the beginning of a new section. Whether it is original or not, the effect of this verse is to emphasize the gravity of the advice which follows.

9–14. This is the first of the major additions which have been made to this Instruction. The consequences of meddling with an adulteress are spelled out in concrete terms very different from the allusive tone of verses 4–6. Verses 9–11 probably refer to the action taken by the woman's husband when he discovers what has been going on. Whether they mean that he obtains heavy damages from the culprit, or that he ruins him by destroying his reputation in the community, the result is the same.

15–20. This is a quite separate treatise on marital fidelity.

15–18. Language connected with *water* is here used to symbolize various aspects of sexual activity. In verses 15 and 18 the *cistern, running water, spring* and *fountain* stand for the sexual satisfaction provided by a wife, with which a man ought to be content. In verse 16 the *well* and *runnels of water*

refer to the male semen: this ought not to be spilled outside the marriage relationship. Behind these metaphors lies
the association of natural with human fertility which was
common to many ancient Near Eastern religions.

19. The second half of this verse (from *Wherever* to the end)
has been transferred here by the N.E.B. translators from 6: 22,
where it does not fit easily into the context.

21. See the note on 15: 3. ✳

MISCELLANEOUS ADVICE

My son, if you pledge yourself to another man	**6**
and stand surety for a stranger,	
if you are caught by your promise,	2
trapped by some promise you have made,	
do what I now tell you*a*	3
and save yourself, my son:	
when you fall into another man's power,	
bestir yourself, go and pester the man,	
give yourself no rest,	4
allow yourself no sleep.	
Save yourself like a gazelle from the toils,*b*	5
like a bird from the grasp of the fowler.	

Go to the ant, you sluggard,	6
watch her ways and get wisdom.	
She has no overseer,	7
no governor or ruler;	
but in summer she prepares her store of food	8
and lays in her supplies at harvest.	
How long, you sluggard, will you lie abed?	9
When will you rouse yourself from sleep?	
A little sleep, a little slumber,	10

[a] what...you: *so Sept.; Heb. has an abbreviated form.*
[b] from the toils: *so Sept.; Heb. out of hand.*

a little folding of the hands in rest,
11 and poverty will come upon you like a robber,
want like a ruffian.

12 A scoundrel, a mischievous man, is he
who prowls about with crooked talk –
13 a wink of the eye,
a touch with the foot,
a sign with the fingers.
14 Subversion is the evil that he is plotting,
he stirs up quarrels all the time.
15 Down comes disaster suddenly upon him;
suddenly he is broken beyond all remedy.

16 Six things the LORD hates,
seven things are detestable to him:
17 a proud eye, a false tongue,
hands that shed innocent blood,
18 a heart that forges thoughts of mischief,
and feet that run swiftly to do evil,
19 a false witness telling a pack of lies,
and one who stirs up quarrels between brothers.

* In this section only verses 1–5 bear some resemblance to the Instruction form, beginning with the phrase *My son* and consisting of direct warnings in the imperative. But they differ from the other Instructions in having no introduction, and they probably did not belong to the original book of ten Instructions.

1–5. A warning against standing surety, that is, giving a pledge or guarantee of someone else's honesty or solvency. Such a pledge would involve a promise to hand over a sum of money or certain goods to a third person if the person guaranteed defaulted. The writer urges anyone who has given such a pledge to go to any lengths to secure his release from it before it is too late.

1. *a stranger*: if this word refers to a foreigner, there may have been a special reason why such a pledge should be demanded: a foreigner might find it difficult to set up in business unless he was vouched for by an Israelite.

3. *bestir yourself*: another possible translation is 'humble yourself' or 'swallow your pride'.

4. Compare *Ahikar*, lines 130–1, on the subject of borrowing: 'Take no rest for yourself until you have paid back the loan.'

6–11. A parable, addressed to the *sluggard*, and based on observation of the industrious activity of the *ant*, which organizes its life most efficiently although it has no master to drive it on. The drawing of lessons from the behaviour of animals was a common feature of wisdom literature in the ancient Near East, and there are other examples in Prov. 30: 24–31. It is possible that the statement in 1 Kings 4: 33 that Solomon 'discoursed of trees, from the cedar of Lebanon down to the marjoram that grows out of the wall, of beasts and birds, of reptiles and fishes' refers to the composition of parables of this kind, although we cannot be certain about this: it may be that this statement refers to some kind of 'scientific' activity.

12–15. On troublemakers. Judging by the frequency of references to such persons both in Proverbs and in non-Israelite wisdom literature, they must have been one of the main curses of the societies of the ancient Near East.

13. There are two possible explanations of these gestures. The man may either be making secret signs to fellow-conspirators or employing magical means in addition to lies to achieve his purpose.

16–19. This type of saying, in which a number of things with common characteristics (here *six...seven*) are listed under the formula 'x/x + 1', also occurs several times in Prov. 30: 15–31 and also in Job 5: 19–22. There is also an example in *Ahikar*, line 92: 'There are two things which are excellent, and three which give pleasure to (the god) Shamash.' The numerical formula itself is also found in non-Israelite epic literature, and elsewhere in the Old Testament (Amos 1: 3–2:8, where the N.E.B. translators have suppressed the Hebrew formula which occurs there eight times – 'For three crimes and for four'). This practice of grouping like things together represents an early stage in the progress of human thought towards a fuller understanding of the world by means of the classification of phenomena; examples of this, known as onomastica, have been found both in Egypt and Mesopotamia.   ✲

AVOID THE ADULTERESS (3)

20 My son, observe your father's commands
   and do not reject the teaching of your mother;

21   wear them always next your heart
   and bind them close about your neck;

23[a]   for a command is a lamp, and teaching a light,
   reproof and correction point the way of life,

24   to keep you from the wife of another man,
   from the seductive tongue of the loose woman.

25   Do not desire her beauty in your heart
   or let her glance provoke you;

26   for a prostitute can be had for the price of a loaf,
   but a married woman is out for bigger game.

27   Can a man kindle fire in his bosom
   without burning his clothes?

28   If a man walks on hot coals,
   will his feet not be scorched?

29   So is he who sleeps with his neighbour's wife;
   no one can touch such a woman and go free.

30   Is not a thief contemptible when he steals
   to satisfy his appetite, even if he is hungry?

31   And, if he is caught, must he not pay seven times over
   and surrender all that his house contains?

[a] *Verse 22 transposed to follow* wrap you round *in 5: 19.*

So one who commits adultery is a senseless fool: 32
he dishonours the woman and ruins himself;
he will get nothing but blows and contumely   33
and will never live down the disgrace;
for a husband's anger is a jealous anger   34
and in the day of vengeance he will show no mercy;
compensation will not buy his forgiveness;[a]   35
no bribe, however large, will purchase his connivance.

* This NINTH INSTRUCTION is similar to 5: 1–23 both in its theme and in the kind of additions which have been made to it. The introduction comprises verses 20–1, and the original Instruction probably consisted of verses 24–5, 32.

21. See the notes on 3: 1–4.

22. This verse has been omitted here by the N.E.B. translators and transferred to 5: 19, on which see the note.

23. This verse is a later addition. The first half seems to be a gloss (that is, an explanation added originally in the margin and later transferred to the text) interpreting the meaning of the words *commands* and *teaching* in verse 20 in terms of a later orthodox Jewish wisdom in which *lamp* and *light* refer to the word of God (compare Ps. 119: 105). The second half, which is similar to Prov. 10: 17, has been added for no obvious reason, perhaps simply to provide the first half with a second line which makes it conform to the rules of Hebrew poetry.

24–5. Compare 2: 16; 5: 3–8; 7: 5, 25.

26. It is clear that the main additional material begins here. The expression translated *married woman* is not the same as that used in verse 24 and its parallels, and the references to the financial consequences of adultery, similar to the additional material in chapter 5, strike a note quite different from that of the original Instructions.

is out for bigger game: literally, 'hunts men's lives'.

[a] compensation...forgiveness: *prob. rdg.; Heb. obscure.*

27–31. A homily on the dangers of adultery. In verses 27–9 it is compared to playing with fire, and in verses 30–1 to theft.

30–1. The point of the comparison between theft and adultery is not clear owing to the difficulty of the text. The N.E.B. translators take the meaning to be that appetite is no excuse for theft, and equally no excuse for adultery. But the analogy of the hungry thief and the lustful man is not a very satisfactory one, and it may be that verse 30 should be translated as a statement rather than a question, and that *And* in verse 31 should be replaced by 'But'. The meaning will then be that a thief has to pay the penalty for his crime even if he has the excuse of hunger; even more so the adulterer, who has no excuse.

31. *seven times over*: this is a more severe penalty for theft than that prescribed in the laws of the Old Testament (Exod. 22: 1–9).

32. *he dishonours the woman and ruins himself*: an alternative translation would be 'he who does so ruins himself'.

33–5. The theme of these verses is the same as that of 5: 9–11. The woman's husband, when he discovers what has been going on, will get his revenge by ruining the culprit. ✳

AVOID THE ADULTERESS (4)

7   My son, keep my words,
     store up my commands in your mind.
2   Keep my commands if you would live,
     and treasure my teaching as the apple of your eye.
3   Wear them like a ring on your finger;
     write them on the tablet of your memory.
4   Call Wisdom your sister,
     greet Understanding as a familiar friend;
5   then they will save you from the adulteress,
     from the loose woman with her seductive words.

I glanced[a] out of the window of my house,   6
I looked down through the lattice,
and I saw among simple youths,   7
there amongst the boys I noticed
a lad, a foolish lad,
passing along the street, at the corner,   8
stepping out in the direction of her house
at twilight, as the day faded,   9
at dusk as the night grew dark;
suddenly a woman came to meet him,   10
dressed like a prostitute, full of wiles,
flighty and inconstant,   11
a woman never content to stay at home,
lying in wait at every corner,   12
now in the street, now in the public squares.
She caught hold of him and kissed him;   13
brazenly she accosted him and said,
'I have had a sacrifice, an offering, to make   14
and I have paid my vows today;
that is why I have come out to meet you,   15
to watch for you and find you.
I have spread coverings on my bed   16
of coloured linen from Egypt.
I have sprinkled my bed with myrrh,   17
my clothes[b] with aloes and cassia.
Come! Let us drown ourselves in pleasure,   18
let us spend a whole night of love;
for the man of the house is away,   19
he has gone on a long journey,
he has taken a bag of silver with him;   20
until the moon is full he will not be home.'

[a] I glanced: *prob. rdg.; Heb. om.*
[b] my clothes: *prob. rdg.; Heb. om.*

43

21 Persuasively she led him on,
she pressed him with seductive words.
22 Like a simple fool he followed her,
like an ox on its way to the slaughter-house,
like an antelope bounding into the noose,
23 like a bird hurrying into the trap;
he did not know that he was risking his life
until the arrow pierced his vitals.

24 But now, my son,[a] listen to me,
attend to what I say.
25 Do not let your heart entice you into her ways,
do not stray down her paths;
26 many has she pierced and laid low,
and her victims are without number.
27 Her house is the entrance to Sheol,
which leads down to the halls of death.

✶ This TENTH AND FINAL INSTRUCTION has, like some of the others, been filled out with additional material; but in this case the additions consist almost entirely of a single independent poem of high literary quality on a similar theme. The original Instruction consisted of verses 1–3, 5, 25–7, which resemble the original Instructions in chapters 2, 5 and 6 very closely in style, vocabulary and length. Into this has been inserted a long self-contained poem consisting of verses 6–23. There are also two other intrusive verses: verse 4 has been introduced for the same reason as 2: 2–4, 10–15; 4: 6–9, 13 to identify the words of the teacher with wisdom. Verse 24 is almost identical with 5: 7, and was probably introduced to bring the reader's attention back to the subject of the original Instruction.

1–3. Compare the introductions to the other Instructions.
2. *the apple of your eye*: literally, 'the little man of your eye.'

[a] my son: *so Sept.; Heb.* O sons.

44

This refers to the pupil of the eye: the phrase is derived from the fact that when we look into someone else's eye we see a 'little man', the reflection of ourselves. The point of the simile is that the teacher's words are as precious as one's eyesight.

4. *sister* here is probably to be taken as meaning 'bride', a usage found in Egyptian. The point of the verse is that the way to safety and happiness is to embrace not the adulteress of the following verse, but Wisdom.

6–23. This is a beautifully constructed poem, full of imaginative description, from the speaker's first glance out of the window to the final similes describing the terrible fate of the foolish young man. The point of view is the same as that of the Instructions, but the literary form and style are quite different. The poem is cast in the form of a personal reminiscence of the teacher and has the character of a parable or cautionary tale. Instead of the brief allusions to the allurements of the adulteress which we find in the Instructions, which leave everything to the imagination, here we have a delight in detailed description. Other features also show that these verses are not part of the original Instruction: the woman here, whether actually a *prostitute* or not, is compared with one (verse 10), whereas this word is never used of the adulteress in the Instructions. We may also note (leaving aside verse 24) that verse 25 does not follow on from verse 23: the woman in verses 6–23 is either a fictitious character or a figure from the past. Thus it does not make sense that the teacher should, in verse 25, warn the pupil not to fall a victim to *her ways*. The *her* clearly refers to the woman of verse 5.

14. *a sacrifice, an offering*: these words apparently refer to the 'shared offering', the regulations for which are found in Lev. 7: 11–36 – one of the few specific references to Israelite customs in the book. The animal was slaughtered in the temple; then, after a portion had been offered to the priest, the remainder was eaten by the worshipper and his family and friends at home. One of the occasions for offering this type of sacrifice was, as here, in fulfilment of a vow previously made

to God when some favour had been sought from him. The regulations required that in such a case the flesh must all be eaten on the same day or the next. The woman makes this the excuse for inviting the young man to her house. It is true that she has already, in verse 13, made it clear that she is inviting him for more than a meal, and some interpreters have thought that the sacrifice in question is not an ordinary Israelite sacrifice but a sexual rite offered to a pagan goddess of love. But there is not really anything in the text which suggests this, and we should be careful not to read too much into it.

19. *the man of the house*: the woman refers to her husband with a contemptuous expression. The theme of the adulteress and the absent husband is drawn from the common stock of Near Eastern wisdom literature. There is a particularly close parallel in *Ani*: 'A woman who is absent from her husband will say to you every day, when she has no witnesses, "I am beautiful." This is a crime worthy of death.'

25-7. Here the Instruction which was broken off after verse 5 is resumed. Two powerful metaphors bring home the deadly effects of association with the adulteress: she is a murderess as surely as if she stabbed her victims in the heart; and *her house* is itself the anteroom to *Sheol*, the abode of the dead, so that anyone who steps into it is already as good as dead. ✷

Wisdom and folly contrasted

THE NATURE AND ORIGINS OF WISDOM

8 Hear how Wisdom lifts her voice
and Understanding cries out.

2 She stands at the cross-roads,
by the wayside, at the top of the hill;

3 beside the gate, at the entrance to the city,
at the entry by the open gate she calls aloud:

'Men, it is to you I call,   4
I appeal to every man:
understand, you simple fools, what it is to be shrewd; 5
you stupid people, understand what sense means.
Listen! For I will speak clearly,   6
you will have plain speech from me;
for I speak nothing but truth   7
and my lips detest wicked talk.
All that I say is right,   8
not a word is twisted or crooked.
All is straightforward to him who can understand,   9
all is plain to the man who has knowledge.
Accept instruction[a] and not silver,   10
knowledge rather than pure gold;
for wisdom is better than red coral,   11
no jewels can match her.
I am Wisdom, I bestow shrewdness   12
and show the way to knowledge and prudence.
[b]Pride, presumption, evil courses,   13
subversive talk, all these I hate.
I have force, I also have ability;   14
understanding and power are mine.
Through me kings are sovereign   15
and governors make just laws.
Through me princes act like princes,   16
from me all rulers on earth[c] derive their nobility.[d]
Those who love me I love,   17
those who search for me find me.
In my hands are riches and honour,   18

[a] *So Sept.; Heb.* my instruction.
[b] *Prob. rdg.; Heb. prefixes* The fear of the LORD is to hate evil.
[c] rulers on earth: *so some MSS.; others* who rule in righteousness.
[d] from me...nobility: *or, with Sept.,* and nobles through me are
rulers on earth.

boundless wealth and the rewards of virtue.

19 My harvest is better than gold, fine gold,
and my revenue better than pure silver.

20 I follow the course of virtue,
my path is the path of justice;

21 I endow with riches those who love me
and I will fill their treasuries.

22 'The LORD created me the beginning of his works,
before all else that he made, long ago.

23 Alone,*a* I was fashioned in times long past,
at the beginning, long before earth itself.

24 When there was yet no ocean I was born,
no springs brimming with water.

25 Before the mountains were settled in their place,
long before the hills I was born,

26 when as yet he had made neither land nor lake
nor the first clod*b* of earth.

27 When he set the heavens in their place I was there,
when he girdled the ocean with the horizon,

28 when he fixed the canopy of clouds overhead
and set the springs of ocean firm in their place,

29 when he prescribed its limits for the sea*c*
and knit together earth's foundations.

30 Then I was at his side each day,
his darling*d* and delight,
playing in his presence continually,

31 playing on the earth, when he had finished it,*e*
while my delight was in mankind.

[a] *So one MS.; others om.*
[b] the first clod: *or* the sum of the clods.
[c] *Prob. rdg.; Heb. adds* and the water shall not disobey his command.
[d] *Or, with Sept.,* craftsman.
[e] the earth...finished it: *prob. rdg., cp. Sept.; Heb.* the world of his earth.

'Now, my sons, listen to me,   32–3
listen to instruction and grow wise, do not reject it.
Happy is the man who keeps to my ways,
happy the man who listens to me,   34
watching daily at my threshold
with his eyes on the doorway;
for he who finds me finds life   35
and wins favour with the LORD,
while he who finds me not, hurts himself,   36
and all who hate me are in love with death.'

✴ This chapter is similar in some ways to 1: 20–33. Wisdom is represented as a woman who offers to instruct any who will listen; and the claims which she makes for her teaching are remarkably similar to those which the teacher makes in the Instructions, so that we have the impression that his teaching has come to life to urge the pupil to pay attention. This personification of Wisdom is a literary device to add vividness to the teaching.

But there are parts of this chapter which are quite different from 1: 20–33. Whereas Wisdom is mainly described without reference to God (in verses 1–21, 32–4, 36), one long passage (verses 22–31) and one other isolated verse (verse 35), together with a short phrase in verse 13 which the N.E.B. has relegated to a footnote, stress the close association between Wisdom and God. These two strands in the poem represent the two stages of theological interpretation which we have observed in our consideration of the book of Instructions.

1–3. Compare 1: 20–1.

1. *Understanding*: simply a synonym for Wisdom. Hebrew poetry regularly repeats the same thought twice in slightly different words.

4. *Men*: characteristically, Wisdom's appeal is universal.

11. Compare 2: 4; 3: 15.

12–21. The way in which Wisdom praises herself in this

49

chapter and especially in these verses has been compared with a type of literature found both in Egypt and Mesopotamia in which a deity speaks of his powers and of the gifts which he will bestow on his worshippers. The similarity is made the more striking by the fact that the deity in question is often a female one. The author of this poem may have been influenced by such literature, but there is emphatically no suggestion that Wisdom has divine status. She is no more than a poetical personification of the teaching of the wisdom teacher or, in verses 22–31, of an attribute of God.

15–16. There was a tradition in the ancient Near East that kings were especially endowed with wisdom. This idea is also found in the Old Testament: in 2 Sam. 14: 17 David's wisdom is compared to that of the angel of God, and in Isa. 11: 2 it is foretold that the spirit of wisdom and understanding will rest on the future king.

17. *Those who love me I love*: Wisdom has already been characterized as a lover or bride (4: 6–8; 7: 4). These passages may have been influenced to some extent by Mesopotamian concepts of the goddess of love, and also perhaps by that of the Egyptian goddess Maat, the goddess of justice. But if so these are no more than literary reminiscences: Wisdom is never deified.

18–21. Although Wisdom has declared that her gifts are of more value than worldly possessions (verses 10–11), this does not mean that she is 'unworldly'. The point is that the man who follows the path of Wisdom will be blessed with every kind of happiness, including that brought by worldly goods, whereas the man who ignores Wisdom and makes only for riches will in the end be disappointed of both.

22–31. These verses develop the teaching of the rest of the chapter by making Wisdom an attribute of God. In order to reinforce his argument the author points out that since God obviously needed wisdom in order to create the world, her connection with him must go back even earlier: he created Wisdom first of all. The brief statement to the same effect in

3 : 19 has here been greatly expanded and put into the mouth of Wisdom herself. As in the other parts of this chapter the author may have derived some of his imagery from non-Israelite mythological sources, but again this is no more than poetic imagery. However, this passage proved to be a crucial one in the development of Wisdom as a theological concept. It exercised a direct influence on Ecclesiasticus (especially chapter 24) and the Wisdom of Solomon (especially chapter 7), two later Jewish wisdom books which now form part of the Apocrypha. These books develop the concept with the help of contemporary mythological and philosophical ideas, raising Wisdom to the status of a distinct 'person', though still subject to God. This in turn led to further developments: Wisdom was identified with the Law, the Word of God and the Spirit of God. Finally the concept of Wisdom as distinct from, and yet one with, the godhead came to play an important part in early Christian theology, especially in the development of the doctrine of the person of Christ. In 1 Cor. 1 : 24, for example, Christ is called 'the wisdom of God', and in Col. 1 : 15–17 his status and functions are described in language which has been in part derived from wisdom terminology.

22. *The LORD created me*: some interpreters hold that the word translated *created* ought to be rendered 'begot'. However, even if this is so there is no sexual connotation: in polytheistic religions in which gods had sexual characteristics 'begot' would have a literal meaning, but in Israel such a meaning would be unthinkable. Yahweh's 'begetting' could only be a metaphor for his act of creation. But it was natural that the pre-existence of Wisdom here should have suggested to Christians the pre-existence of Christ and his relationship to his Father. This passage may have been in the mind of the author of the fourth Gospel when he wrote, 'The Word, then, was with God at the beginning, and through him all things came to be; no single thing was created without him' (John 1 : 2–3).

23–6. Great emphasis is laid here on the priority in time of the creation of wisdom by God. The author uses the vocabulary of current creation traditions, naming each created element in turn. The idea that the *mountains were settled* in the midst of the sea on pillars is found elsewhere in the Old Testament, for example in Job 9: 6; 38: 6; Ps. 18: 7; 104: 5–6.

24. *born*: here and in verse 25 this word is used metaphorically of Wisdom's creation by God.

27–30. Having stated that Wisdom was created before the world, the author now goes a step further: Wisdom was actually present when the subsequent acts of creation were performed.

30. *his darling and delight*: the picture is of a child playing by its father's side. There has been much controversy about the word translated *darling*: some scholars believe that the Septuagint is correct in taking it to mean 'craftsman'. If this were correct, it would mean that Wisdom actively assisted God in the design and execution of the creation of the world.

31. *my delight was in mankind*: the author ends his interpolated poem by returning to the subject with which the chapter as a whole is concerned.

32–6. If verses 22–31 are an interpolation, verse 32 ought to be the continuation of verse 21. But verses 32–6 have suffered some disarrangement, and some additions have been made to the original. The restoration of their original form is a disputed problem, but certain points are clear. This is the only place where Wisdom addresses mankind as *my sons*; such a form of address would be more suitable to the human wisdom teacher. Further, the second line of verse 35 is of the same kind as verses 22–31, introducing a connection between Wisdom and God into a passage where no such connection was originally made.

34. The references to Wisdom's *threshold* and *doorway* suggest the house of the wisdom teacher where he gives his instruction; but there is also a deliberate contrast with the house of the adulterous woman (5: 8; 7: 27): the one leads to death, the other to life. This contrast is made even more vividly in chapter 9.   ❋

WISDOM AND THE LADY STUPIDITY

Wisdom has built her house,   **9**
she has hewn her seven pillars;
she has killed a beast and spiced her wine,   2
and she has spread her table.
She has sent out her maidens to proclaim   3
from the highest part of the town,
'Come in, you simpletons.'   4
She says also to the fool,
'Come, dine with me   5
and taste the wine that I have spiced.
Cease to be silly, and you will live,   6
you will grow in understanding.'

Correct an insolent man, and be sneered at for your pains; 7
  correct a bad man, and you will put yourself in the
    wrong.
Do not correct the insolent or they will hate you;   8
correct a wise man, and he will be your friend.
Lecture a wise man, and he will grow wiser;   9
teach a righteous man, and his learning will increase.

The first step to wisdom is the fear of the LORD,   10
  and knowledge of the Holy One is understanding;
for through me your days will be multiplied   11
and years will be added to your life.
If you are wise, it will be to your own advantage;   12
if you are haughty, you alone are to blame.
The Lady Stupidity is a flighty creature;   13
the simpleton, she cares for nothing.
She sits at the door of her house,   14
on a seat in the highest part of the town,
to invite the passers-by indoors   15

as they hurry on their way:

16 'Come in, you simpletons', she says.
She says also to the fool,

17 'Stolen water is sweet
and bread got by stealth tastes good.'

18 Little does he know that death[a] lurks there,
that her guests are in the depths of Sheol.

✳ Chapter 9 contains three distinct sections: verses 1–6, 7–12, 13–18. The first and third of these clearly belong to one another: they make a contrast, carried even into the details, between the invitations made by Wisdom and by the 'woman of foolishness' (somewhat flamboyantly rendered *The Lady Stupidity* in the N.E.B.) to the *simpletons* or impressionable young men to enter their houses and share their feasts. Verses 7–12 were originally unconnected with the rest of the chapter, and their insertion here weakens the contrast between the other two sections.

1–6. Here Wisdom is represented as a woman who has *built her house* and invites all and sundry to the housewarming. Behind this image lie reminiscences of the invitations of the wisdom teachers in the Instructions, and also of the earlier invitation of Wisdom herself in chapter 8 (note especially the similarity with 8: 34).

1. Some interpreters have read a deep significance into Wisdom's *house* with its *seven pillars*, associating this verse with the supposed references to Wisdom's part in the creation of the world in 8: 22–31, and suggesting that the house and pillars have a cosmological significance representing Wisdom as the architect of the universe. But more probably the seven pillars were simply a feature of palatial residences of the period.

2–5. The feast here is a feast of Wisdom which fulfils its promise to give life, contrasted with the surreptitious and illusory pleasures offered by the Lady Stupidity (verse 17), which lead to death.

[a] *Lit.* the majority (*that is* the dead).

7–12. These interpolated verses consist of a number of short units partly grouped according to their subjects. They are uncharacteristic of this section of Proverbs, but similar (apart from verse 10, on which see the note) to material in other parts of the book. Compare especially 15: 5, 10, 12, 32.

7–9. These three sayings, which share a common theme, are somewhat pessimistic in tone: in contrast to the rather optimistic assumption of verses 1–6 that even fools may accept Wisdom's invitation, they point out that there are some people – the *insolent* and the *bad* – who are incapable of profiting by her teaching, and that it is better not to try to reason with them.

10. See the note on 1: 7. The insertion of this verse is intended to give a religious interpretation to the contrast between Wisdom and the Lady Stupidity: to accept the invitation of the latter is to abandon the *fear of the LORD* in favour of false religion.

11. *through me*: this only makes sense if Wisdom is speaking. It may be intended to give the impression that these verses are the continuation of Wisdom's speech in verses 3–6. On the other hand the phrase is inconsistent with verse 10, in which Wisdom is spoken of in a way which shows that she is not the speaker.

13–18. *The Lady Stupidity* (literally, 'woman of foolishness') is a composite figure. The phrase occurs only here, and this is an indication that she is not simply to be identified with the adulteress of the Instructions. The adulteress is a typical figure standing for real, live adulteresses in general: the adultery into which she tempts the young fool is real adultery. But *the Lady Stupidity* is a symbolic figure, offering a parallel to the equally symbolic figure of Wisdom. Between them, in this chapter, Wisdom and Stupidity offer a choice between two ways of life: they dramatize the teaching of the wisdom teacher with its doctrine of the Two Ways (4: 10–19). It is in order to bring out this contrast that the invitations of the two female figures are expressed in such similar terms. But *the Lady Stupidity* does have some of the characteristics of an adulteress: it is clearly an adulterous relationship to which she invites the young man. In this case, however, adultery is mainly a symbol for wilful folly in general. The author of this passage has used the literal warnings against adultery and made them into a symbol of something more fundamental.

14. *sits at the door of her house*: this is a familiar posture of prostitutes; but there may also be a reference to a feature of a specific sexual cult of the goddess of love practised in Babylonia.

17. This is probably a popular proverb.

18. Compare similar statements in 2: 18–19; 7: 27. This is the most dramatic of these statements, and makes a fitting ending to this section of the book. ✳

SECTION II. PROVERBS 10:1–22:16

A collection of wise sayings

Chapters 10: 1–22: 16 consist of a collection of short sayings, each of which expresses a complete thought and, with few exceptions, corresponds to a single verse in the text. A modern editor would probably have arranged them in sections according to their subjects. Some indications of such an arrangement are occasionally apparent: for example, 16: 10–15 (apart from verse 11) are all about kings. In some other cases a mnemonic, that is, memory-helping, purpose seems to have been at work, suggesting that parts of this collection may once have been learned by heart: 18: 20–2, for example, all begin with the same Hebrew letter. Probably other associations of ideas and of sounds played their part in determining the order in which the sayings are placed; but as far, at least, as the modern reader can see the great majority have no significant arrangement.

This section, like chapters 1-9, was not composed all at once. Some sayings occur twice: for example, 14: 12 is identical with 16: 25. This suggests that several smaller collections have been combined, and that when this was done duplicate material was allowed to stand. But the very existence of the same sayings in two originally different collections further suggests that there may have been a common stock of sayings which could be drawn upon.

The majority of the sayings in this section are in the statement form rather than that of the Instruction (see p. 6). This form, in which life-situations are described with no comment (e.g. 'A soft answer turns away anger', 15: 1; 'stupid men talk nonsense', 15: 2), corresponds to Mesopotamian (and probably Canaanite) wisdom literature rather than to Egyptian. In spite of its form its purpose is no less to instruct than in the case of the formal 'Instruction'.

Most of these sayings fall into one or another of a fairly small number of formal patterns which reveal something of their purpose and of ancient Near Eastern patterns of thought. Some of the most frequently occurring patterns will be described here; others will be pointed out in the commentary.

1. *Antithetical parallelism*. This simply means that the same thought is stated twice, but in two contrasting ways, e.g.:

> A wise son brings joy to his father;
> a foolish son is his mother's bane.   (10: 1)

> Diligence brings a man to power,
> but laziness to forced labour.   (12: 24)

Such contrasts reveal a tendency to judge human behaviour in terms of black and white. This tendency is related to the concept of a universal Order, conformity to which is the basic criterion of conduct.

2. *Synonymous parallelism*. Here also the thought is stated twice, but there is no contrast: it is simply put in different words, e.g.:

Pride comes before disaster,
and arrogance before a fall.   (16:18)

A false witness will not escape punishment,
and one who utters nothing but lies will perish.   (19:9)

This habit of repetition is characteristic of much of the poetry
of the Old Testament and also of that of the ancient Near East.
Probably it was felt that the repetition of the same thought in
similar but not identical language gave it greater comprehen-
siveness, and so greater validity and authority. A glance at the
Psalms will show how frequently these patterns were used.
In the following quotation, for example, the first two lines are
in synonymous, and the last two in antithetic, parallelism:

Great is the LORD and worthy of all praise;
    he is more to be feared than all gods.
    For the gods of the nations are idols every one;
    but the LORD made the heavens.   (Ps. 96:4–5)

3. *The continuous sentence.* In many cases there is no repetition: the thought was too long for a single line, and ran on
into the second, e.g.:

A strong man who trusts in the fear of the LORD
will be a refuge for his sons.   (14:26)

A wicked man accepts a bribe under his cloak
to pervert the course of justice.   (17:23)

Here, although there is no parallelism, the twofold shape of
the saying is preserved.

4. *Comparisons.* Not everything was seen in terms of black
and white. Man's progress towards a better understanding of
his world involved the making of comparisons and of comparative value-judgements. This section of the book contains
a number of different types of comparison, e.g.:

Like a gold ring in a pig's snout
is a beautiful woman without good sense.   (11:22)

> If the righteous in the land get their deserts,
> how much more the wicked man and the sinner!
>
> $$(11:31)$$

5. *Statement and explanation.* In some cases the first line makes a statement and the second explains its meaning:

> A king's threat is like a lion's roar;
> one who ignores it is his own worst enemy.   (20: 2)

It is possible that in some of these cases the explanatory second line was added to an originally shorter saying.

Theological development is much more difficult to detect in this section than in chapters 1–9. But there are some indications of a re-interpretation of older wisdom teaching in terms of the specifically Israelite religious tradition. For example, the following two sayings are identical except for the initial phrase:

> *A wise man's teaching* is a fountain of life
> for one who would escape the snares of death.   (13: 14)

> *The fear of the LORD* is the fountain of life
> for the man who would escape the snares of death.
>
> $$(14:27)$$

It is difficult to avoid the conclusion that the second of these is a 'theological' interpretation of the first.

THE PROVERBS of Solomon: **10**

> A wise son brings joy to his father;
> a foolish son is his mother's bane.
> Ill-gotten wealth brings no profit;   2
> uprightness is a safeguard against death.
> The LORD does not let the righteous go hungry,[a]   3
> but he disappoints the cravings[b] of the wicked.
> Idle hands make a man poor;   4

[a] *Or* be afraid.   [b] *Or* the clamour.

busy hands grow rich.

5 A thoughtful son puts by in summer;
a son who sleeps at harvest is a disgrace.

6 Blessings are showered on the righteous;
the wicked are choked by their own violence.

7 The righteous are remembered in blessings;
the name of the wicked turns rotten.

8 A wise man takes a command to heart;
a foolish talker comes to grief.

9 A blameless life makes for security;
crooked ways bring a man down.

10 To wink at a fault causes trouble;
a frank rebuke leads to peace.*a*

11 The words of good men are a fountain of life;
the wicked are choked by their own violence.

12 Hate is always picking a quarrel,
but love turns a blind eye to every fault.

13 The man of understanding has wisdom on his lips;
a rod is in store for the back of the fool.

14 Wise men lay up knowledge;
when a fool speaks, ruin is near.

15 A rich man's wealth is his strong city,
but poverty is the undoing of the helpless.

16 The good man's labour is his livelihood;
the wicked man's earnings bring him to a bad end.

17 Correction is the high road to life;
neglect reproof and you miss the way.

18 There is no spite in a just man's*b* talk;
it is the stupid who are fluent with calumny.

19 When men talk too much, sin is never far away;

[a] a frank...peace: *so Sept.; Heb.* a foolish talker comes to grief,
cp. verse 8.
[b] a just man's: *so Sept.; Heb.* lying.

common sense holds its tongue.

A good man's tongue is pure silver;   20
the heart of the wicked is trash.

The lips of a good man teach[a] many,   21
but fools perish for want of sense.

The blessing of the LORD brings riches   22
and he sends no sorrow with them.

Lewdness is sport for the stupid;   23
wisdom a delight to men of understanding.

The fears of the wicked will overtake them;   24
the desire of the righteous will be granted.

When the whirlwind has passed by, the wicked are 25
gone;
the foundations of the righteous are eternal.

Like vinegar on the teeth or smoke in the eyes,   26
so is the lazy servant to his master.

The fear of the LORD brings length of days;   27
the years of the wicked are few.

The hope of the righteous blossoms;   28
the expectation of the wicked withers away.

The way of the LORD gives refuge to the honest man, 29
but dismays those who do evil.

The righteous man will never be shaken;   30
the wicked shall not remain on earth.

Wisdom flows from the mouth of the righteous;   31
the subversive tongue will be rooted out.

The righteous man can suit his words to the occasion; 32
the wicked know only subversive talk.

✻ 1. *The proverbs of Solomon*: although it would be rash to claim that any of the sayings in this section come from Solomon himself, some of them may well come from his time.

[a] *Prob. rdg., cp. Vulg.; Heb.* nourish.

A wise son: the educational theme is no less prominent in this section than in chapters 1–9. Antithetical parallelism is particularly frequent in chapters 10–15.

2. *Ill-gotten wealth*: wealth is another frequent theme in this section. Mainly it is regarded with approval as the just reward of righteousness (so verse 22); but the wisdom writers were realistic enough to know that some wealth was ill-gotten. Their answer to the problem posed by this fact was that such wealth could not protect its possessor against eventual divine punishment: so in the end it *brings no profit*.

a safeguard against death: this is not a promise of eternal life. The meaning is that the reward of *uprightness* is a long and happy life.

3. The view that men ultimately get what they deserve is expressed sometimes in terms of a personal action of God, as here, and sometimes in impersonal terms which imply the existence of a just Order, as in verse 2.

4–5. Laziness and diligence constitute another frequent theme. It is assumed throughout the book that all men, whatever their station in life, are expected to work. There are no 'idle rich': even kings and courtiers have their proper job to do.

5. No difference in meaning is intended between *summer* and *harvest*: harvesting was done in what we should call the autumn, but which in Hebrew terminology was included in the 'summer'.

6–7. Two sayings on *blessings*, the *righteous* and the *wicked*.

7. It was the hope of every Israelite that he would be *remembered* for the good which he had done and that his *name*, that is, his good reputation, would endure permanently. A belief in personal survival after death only arose much later – probably during the second century B.C.; but the survival of a man's *name* represented a kind of prolongation of his life, and so was very important to him.

8. In its teaching about the proper use of speech and the necessity for taking good advice, Proverbs follows the wisdom

tradition of the ancient Near East. Here a contrast is drawn between the man who pays attention to the *command*, or advice, of the wisdom teacher and the man who makes a fool of himself by giving advice when he himself is ignorant.

9. *crooked ways*: on the metaphor of the way see 4: 10–19.

10–14. Five sayings on the right and wrong use of speech.

10. *To wink at a fault*: the Hebrew has simply 'winking the eye', almost the same phrase as in 6: 13, where it has nothing to do with overlooking faults. It may be that this line refers to the man who causes trouble by telling lies, while winking to those who are 'in the know'.

11. *a fountain of life*: that is, a spring of 'living' or life-giving water, which was naturally more highly valued than rainwater collected in cisterns, the only source of supply in places where there was no natural spring. But 'life' also stands for all that is sound and healthy: the meaning is that a good man's words contribute to the well-being of the community. The second line is identical with verse 6*b* (see pp. 2–3).

12. *love* and *hate* here refer to social relationships: the thought is the same as in Lev. 19: 18: 'You shall not seek revenge, or cherish anger towards your kinsfolk; you shall love your neighbour as a man like yourself', a text which was singled out by Jesus as one of the two greatest commandments in the Law (Matt. 22: 39 and parallels).

15–16. Two sayings about *wealth*.

15. *his strong city*: wealth protects a man from misfortune just as a strongly fortified capital protects a king from his enemies.

16. *is his livelihood*: literally, 'is for life'; *bring him to a bad end*: literally, 'are for sin'. The N.E.B. translators have taken 'sin' to be the equivalent of 'death' (compare 11: 19). But possibly 'sin' ought to be taken literally: the saying would then be making a contrast between the ways in which the two types of man use their money.

17–21. Five more sayings about speech.

17. *Correction*: that is, scholastic or parental discipline.

18. In the first line the N.E.B. follows the Septuagint. The Hebrew has 'He who conceals hatred has lying lips', making a synonymous rather than an antithetical parallelism. The line would then refer to the smooth talker who conceals his evil intentions.

19. *sin*: an alternative translation would be 'offence'.

22. *riches*: that is, material wealth, were one of the normal rewards of righteousness according to ancient Near Eastern belief. Unlike the *ill-gotten wealth* of the wicked (see verse 2), the wealth which comes with God's *blessing* is unalloyed.

24–5. Two sayings contrasting the fates of the *wicked* and the *righteous*.

26. There is no subtle meaning hidden behind this simple observation: its sole purpose is to express an obvious truth in an entertaining way.

27–32. Each of these six sayings concerns itself with the *righteous* or *honest man* and his opposite. In two of them (verses 27 and 29) the fates of these two types of men are settled by God; in the others it is the impersonal Order which decides their fates.

27. *The fear of the LORD*: see the note on 1: 7.

29. *The way of the LORD*: elsewhere in the Old Testament this phrase means 'Yahweh's commandments'. The idea of a way giving refuge is a somewhat strange one. A very slight alteration of the text would give the line 'The LORD gives refuge to the man of honest ways'.

30. *on earth*: as in 2: 21 an alternative translation would be 'in the land', referring to the land of Canaan which had been given to Israel on condition of good behaviour.

32. *suit his words to the occasion*: the N.E.B. translation might suggest that glibness of speech is a characteristic of *the righteous man*; but the real meaning is that *the righteous man* uses his words constructively, to pour oil on troubled waters, in contrast the to *subversive talk* of *the wicked*. ✶

False scales are the LORD's abomination; **11**
correct weights are dear to his heart.
When presumption comes in, in comes contempt, 2
but wisdom goes with sagacity.
Honesty is a guide to the upright, 3
but rogues are balked by their own perversity.
Wealth is worth nothing in the day of wrath, 4
but uprightness is a safeguard against death.
By uprightness the blameless keep their course, 5
but the wicked are brought down by their wickedness.
Uprightness saves the righteous, 6
but rogues are trapped in their own[a] greed.
When a man[b] dies, his thread of life ends, 7
and with it ends the hope of affluence.
A righteous man is rescued from disaster, 8
and the wicked man plunges into it.
By his words a godless man tries to ruin others, 9
but they are saved when the righteous plead for them.
A city rejoices in the prosperity of the righteous; 10
there is jubilation when the wicked perish.
By the blessing of the upright a city is built up; 11
the words of the wicked tear it down.
A man without sense despises others, 12
but a man of understanding holds his peace.
A gossip gives away secrets, 13
but a trusty man keeps his own counsel.
For want of skilful strategy an army is lost; 14
victory is the fruit of long planning.
Give a pledge for a stranger and know no peace; 15
refuse to stand surety and be safe.
Grace in a woman wins honour, 16

[a] their own: *so Sept.; Heb. om.*
[b] a man: *so some MSS.; others* a wicked man.

but she who hates virtue makes a home for dishonour.
Be timid in business and come to beggary;[a]
be bold and make a fortune.

17 Loyalty brings its own reward;
a cruel man makes trouble for his kin.

18 A wicked man earns a fallacious[b] profit;
he who sows goodness reaps a sure reward.[c]

19 A man set on righteousness finds life,
but the pursuit of evil leads to death.

20 The LORD detests the crooked heart,
but honesty is dear to him.

21 Depend upon it:[d] an evil man shall not escape
punishment;
the righteous and all their offspring shall go free.

22 Like a gold ring in a pig's snout
is a beautiful woman without good sense.

23 The righteous desire only what is good;
the hope of the wicked comes to nothing.

24 A man may spend freely and yet grow richer;
another is sparing beyond measure, yet ends in poverty.

25 A generous man grows fat and prosperous,
and he who refreshes others will himself be refreshed.[e]

26 He who withholds his grain is cursed by the people,
but he who sells his corn is blessed.

27 He who eagerly seeks what is good finds much favour,
but if a man pursues evil it turns upon him.

28 Whoever relies on his wealth is riding for a fall,
but the righteous flourish like the green leaf.

29 He who brings trouble on his family inherits the wind,

[a] but she...beggary: *so Sept.; Heb. om.*
[b] *Or* fraudulent.
[c] a sure reward: *or* the reward of honesty.
[d] Depend upon it: *lit.* Hand on hand.
[e] will himself be refreshed: *prob. rdg., cp. Vulg.; Heb. unintelligible.*

and a fool becomes slave to a wise man.
The fruit of righteousness is a tree of life,　　　　30
but violence*a* means the taking away of life.
If the righteous in the land get their deserts,　　　　31
how much more the wicked man and the sinner!

✳ 1. Although there is a law in Deut. 25: 13–16 on this subject expressed in very similar terms, including the phrase *the LORD's abomination*, there is probably no direct connection between the two passages. A similar crime is condemned in *Amen-em-opet* XVII 18: 23 – 19: 1 as 'abomination to (the god) Re'. Giving short weight either by tinkering with the scales or by using false weights was a practice frequently condemned in ancient Near Eastern laws, and in the Old Testament it is condemned also by the prophets Micah (6:11) and Amos (8: 5).

2. *sagacity*: 'modesty' would perhaps be a better translation.

3–6. Four sayings about the rewards of *uprightness*.

4. *the day of wrath*: this refers to the punishment which will inevitably befall every wicked man in his lifetime. There is no reference here to a judgement after death. The second line is identical with 10: 2*b*, and the point of both sayings is the same.

7. *When a man dies*: almost all the Hebrew manuscripts have 'When a *wicked* man dies'. This might imply that for the righteous man there is a life after death, a doctrine otherwise unknown to Proverbs. The manuscripts followed by the N.E.B. express the normal teaching of the Old Testament.

9. *when the righteous plead for them*: literally, 'by the knowledge of the righteous'. Knowledge is the equivalent of wisdom, and wisdom enables a righteous man to see through the godless man's designs and to thwart them.

10–11. The keyword here is *city*: the common theme is the relationship between the individual and the community.

[*a*] *So Sept.; Heb.* a wise man.

11. *the blessing of the upright*: the divine favour granted to upright citizens is not confined to them alone, but spreads to the whole city; conversely the wicked members of a community could bring about its ruin. The Israelites, together with other peoples of the ancient Near East, believed profoundly that the actions of the individual cannot help affecting and being affected by others.

12. *without sense*: literally, 'deficient in heart'. The heart was believed to be the seat of the intelligence: see the note on 4:23.

13. *gossip*: the word usually means 'slander'. But gossip, even if true, can be just as injurious to a person's reputation as lying slander. No society can hang together unless confidences are respected. The same teaching is found in *Amen-em-opet*.

14. *skilful strategy*: the Hebrew word's literal meaning is 'seamanship': the metaphor is the same as in the expression 'steering the ship of state'. The word translated *army* usually means 'nation'.

long planning: literally, 'an abundance of counsellors'. For the function of the counsellor at court see 2 Sam. 16: 20–17: 14. Ahithophel is called 'David's counsellor' in 2 Sam. 15: 12. This verse illustrates the court connections of the wisdom literature.

15. Compare 6: 1–5 and see the notes on that passage.

16. The Hebrew text of this verse contains only the first and the last lines. Translated somewhat differently these make some kind of sense: 'A gracious woman wins honour, and a violent man wins riches.' The verb is the same in each line. The N.E.B. follows the Septuagint, which has two extra lines; and these certainly improve the parallelism. In cases such as these it is always difficult to say whether the longer text is the original, and has been accidentally mutilated at some stage in the copying of the text, or whether the supplementary material is a later addition made in order to produce better sense.

17. *his kin*: an alternative translation would be 'himself'.

18–21. Four sayings contrasting the fates of the *wicked* and the *righteous*.

20. *The LORD detests*: this is the same phrase in Hebrew as 3: 32; 11: 1, on which see the notes.

21. *Depend upon it*: literally, 'hand on hand'. The expression is derived from the practice of striking hands to conclude a bargain, and so means that the thing is settled.

and all their offspring: it is not clear why the descendants of the *righteous* are specifically mentioned, unless it is to emphasize that they will be rewarded with children while the *evil man* will suffer the additional punishment of childlessness. On the other hand the Hebrew word translated *offspring* sometimes refers not to children but to a class of people: 'the righteous and all their kind'. The N.E.B. translators themselves render it in that way in Isa. 1: 4.

22. This rather inelegant comparison, like 10: 26 which it resembles in form, may be a popular saying.

24–6. Three sayings about generosity and meanness.

24. This verse is capable of more than one interpretation: it may mean that things do not always turn out as one might expect, or its meaning may be similar to that of verse 25: generosity brings its own reward, while meanness does not pay in the end. We must always reckon with the possibility that the ambiguity in some of these sayings may be deliberate.

25. *generous man*: literally, 'person of blessing'. This phrase could equally mean 'a person who has received divine favour'.

26. The situation envisaged here is a time of famine. It is the moral duty of the rich man who has corn stored up from previous years to put it on the market. The reason why he might refuse to do this is not stated; but it may be implied that he holds out as long as possible in order to force the price up, unmoved by the people's suffering.

27. *finds much favour*: the usual translation of this verb is not 'find' but 'seek'. A meaning such as 'finds' or 'obtains' seems to be necessary if the saying is to make good sense, but the commentators disagree about how such a meaning can be obtained. It is also not clear whether *favour* here means God's approval or man's.

28. *is riding for a fall*: the N.E.B. translation is much more elaborate than the original, which simply has 'will fall'!

like the green leaf: a frequent symbol of prosperity both in the Old Testament and other ancient Near Eastern religious literature. The relationship between the fertility of the crops and human prosperity was an idea common to many of the religions of that region, and came to be a commonplace in poetry.

29. *brings trouble*: the translation of the N.E.B. is vague because the exact meaning of the Hebrew is not known. The verse is difficult in other ways. *family* could equally well be translated as 'household', referring to the man's property, which suffers damage in some way, rather than to his relations. If this is so the reference may be to incompetence in business: as a result of his folly the man finds that his inheritance is nothing but *wind*, that is, valueless; and so he has to sell himself as a slave to the *wise man*, who has successfully managed his affairs. But the interpretation of the verse is uncertain.

30. To call a *fruit* a *tree* is a careless metaphor, but the meaning is clear: righteousness receives as its reward 'life', that is, happiness of every kind. The metaphor of the *tree of life* has a mythological background. Its use here does not necessarily mean that the author specifically had in mind Gen. 2:9; 3:22, where the fruit of the tree of life confers eternal life, but has been placed out of man's reach. The author of this verse may have known the myth in a different form. It is certainly not eternal life of which he was thinking.

violence: the Hebrew has 'a wise man', which makes no sense. The N.E.B. translators have substituted a similar word meaning 'violence'. *taking away of life* then becomes an elaborate way of referring to death.

31. Once more there is no reference here to judgement after death: it is in this life that we shall get our deserts. The author seems to be more certain about the fate of the wicked than about that of the righteous; but the expression *how much more* is perhaps not to be taken literally. ✳

He who loves correction loves knowledge;   **12**
he who hates reproof is a mere brute.

A good man earns favour from the Lord;   2
the schemer is condemned.

No man can establish himself by wickedness,   3
but good men have roots that cannot be dislodged.

A capable wife is her husband's crown;   4
one who disgraces him is like rot in his bones.

The purposes of the righteous are lawful;   5
the designs of the wicked are full of deceit.

The wicked are destroyed[a] by their own words;   6
ths words of the good man are his salvation.

Once the wicked are down, that is the end of them,   7
but the good man's line continues.

A man is commended for his intelligence,   8
but a warped mind is despised.

It is better to be modest[b] and earn one's living   9
than to be conceited[c] and go hungry.

A righteous man cares for his beast,   10
but a wicked man is cruel at heart.

He who tills his land has enough to eat,   11
but to follow idle pursuits is foolishness.

The stronghold of the wicked crumbles like clay,[d]   12
but the righteous take lasting root.

The wicked man is trapped by his own falsehoods,   13
but the righteous comes safe through trouble.

One man wins success by his words;   14
another gets his due reward by the work of his hands.

A fool thinks that he is always right;   15

[a] *Prob. rdg.; Heb.* are an ambush for blood.
[b] *Or* scorned.
[c] *Or* honoured.
[d] *Prob. rdg.; Heb.* A wicked man covets a stronghold of crumbling earth.

wise is the man who listens to advice.

16 A fool shows his ill humour at once;
   a clever man slighted conceals his feelings.

17 An honest speaker comes out with the truth,
   but the false witness is full of deceit.

18 Gossip can be sharp as a sword,
   but the tongue of the wise heals.

19 Truth spoken stands firm for ever,
   but lies live only for a moment.

20 Those who plot evil delude themselves,
   but there is joy for those who seek the common
      good.

21 No mischief will befall the righteous,
   but wicked men get their fill of adversity.

22 The Lord detests a liar
   but delights in the honest man.

23 A clever man conceals his knowledge,
   but a stupid man broadcasts his folly.

24 Diligence brings a man to power,
   but laziness to forced labour.

25 An anxious heart dispirits a man,
   and a kind word fills him with joy.

26 A righteous man recoils from evil,*a*
   but the wicked take a path that leads them astray.

27 The lazy hunter puts up no game,
   but the industrious man reaps a rich harvest.*b*

28 The way of honesty leads to life,
   but there is a well-worn path to death.

* 1. The point of this saying is that education is useless
without the active participation of the pupil.

[a] recoils from evil: *prob. rdg.; Heb.* let him spy out his friend.
[b] but...harvest: *prob. rdg.; Heb. obscure.*

4. *A capable wife*: the qualities of the capable wife are set out in detail in 31: 10–31.

rot in his bones: this striking phrase, which recurs in 14: 30, well expresses the steady deterioration of a man cursed with an incapable or irresponsible wife who *disgraces* him, that is, who lowers his standing in the community. Another example of the comparison of physical distress with mental anguish is found in 10: 26.

5–7. Three sayings contrasting the *good man* with the *wicked*.

6. *are destroyed*: the Hebrew (see the footnote) seems to mean that the wicked seek to destroy others by the things which they say. The N.E.B. translators, on the grounds that this does not yield a suitable parallelism with the next line, have slightly altered the text to mean that it is the wicked who destroy themselves. It is possible, however, to make sense of the Hebrew as its stands: the wicked set a trap for the good man by making false accusations, but the good man, strengthened by the divine blessing which is his, is enabled to escape the trap by making a skilful defence.

7. *the good man's line*: literally, 'the good man's house'. This word can mean 'family', that is, descendants; if so, the saying means that the good man will be blessed with posterity but the wicked man will be deprived of it. Alternatively the word may mean 'household' in the sense of material possessions: if so, the meaning is similar to that of the parable of the two houses in Matt. 7: 24–7.

10. *cares for his beast*: that kindness should be shown to animals as well as to human beings was recognized also in the laws of the Old Testament, e.g.: 'You shall not muzzle an ox while it is treading out the corn' (Deut. 25: 4).

12–13. Two more sayings on the fates of the *wicked* and the *righteous*.

12. The first line hardly makes sense in the Hebrew (see the footnote). The rendering of the N.E.B. is based on a rather drastic emendation of the text.

14. *One man...another*: no contrast is intended here. The point is that we shall receive the due reward both of our good words and of our good deeds.

15–16. Two sayings contrasting the *wise* man and the *fool*. Accepting good advice (compare verse 1) and concealing one's feelings are two of the main elements in the teaching of ancient Near Eastern wisdom literature.

16. *his feelings*: the Hebrew has 'an insult'.

17–19. Three more sayings on good and evil speech.

17. We should not dismiss sayings such as this as worthless because they state what is obvious. The purpose of this saying is to condemn the giving of false evidence as it is condemned in the Old Testament laws (e.g. Exod. 20: 16). But if the statement form of wisdom saying is used, this is the only way of putting it. If the Instruction form had been used, this saying might have been something like 'Speak the truth in honesty, and avoid the deceit of the false witness'.

19. *Truth spoken*: literally, 'the lip of truth'. Compare *Ptah-hotep*'s 'Truth is good and of permanent value.' The point is that truth belongs to the fundamental Order of the world, and can therefore not be obscured by lies for more than a moment: 'truth will out'.

20. *seek the common good*: compare 11: 10–11 and the notes on those verses.

22. *The LORD detests*: on this phrase see the note on 3: 32. Compare also *Amen-em-opet* x 13: 15–16:

> Do not speak falsehood to any man:
> it is the abomination of God.

24. *brings a man to power*: not necessarily in a political sense, although this is not excluded. The contrast is between the man who works hard and rises to the top and the lazy man who will inevitably sink to the bottom. *forced labour* if strictly interpreted refers to a form of oppression which was suffered by Israel in Egypt and again under Solomon; but here it probably refers to slavery in general.

26. *recoils from evil*: the Hebrew of this line is difficult (see the footnote), and the N.E.B. translation is one of a number based on attempts to correct the text.

27. The Hebrew of this verse also is difficult. The only thing of which we can be certain is that there is a contrast between the *lazy* and the *industrious man*, and that the first line has to do with hunting.

28. In this saying the meaning of the first line is clear, but the second is obscure. An alternative rendering might be 'but the way of folly leads to death'. In any case this is a further example of the doctrine of the Two Ways, on which see the notes on 4: 10–19. *life*, as in other passages, signifies happiness and prosperity in this life. ✳

A wise man sees the reason for his father's correction;   **I3**
    an arrogant man will not listen to rebuke.
A good man enjoys the fruit of righteousness,[a]   2
    but violence is meat and drink for the treacherous.
He who minds his words preserves his life;   3
    he who talks too much comes to grief.
A lazy man is torn by appetite unsatisfied,   4
    but the diligent grow fat and prosperous.
The righteous hate falsehood;   5
    the doings of the wicked are foul and deceitful.
To do right is the protection of an honest man,   6
    but wickedness brings sinners to grief.[b]
One man pretends to be rich, although he has   7
    nothing;
    another has great wealth but goes in rags.[c]
A rich man must buy himself off,   8

[a] righteousness: *so Sept.; Heb.* a man's mouth.
[b] brings...grief: *or* plays havoc with a man.
[c] One man...rags: *or* One man may grow rich though he has nothing; another may grow poor though he has great wealth.

but a poor man is immune from threats.

9 The light of the righteous burns brightly;
the embers of the wicked will be put out.

10 A brainless fool causes strife by his presumption;
wisdom is found among friends in council.

11 Wealth quickly come by[a] dwindles away,
but if it comes little by little, it multiplies.

12 Hope deferred makes the heart sick;
a wish come true is a staff of life.

13 To despise a word of advice is to ask for trouble;
mind what you are told, and you will be rewarded.

14 A wise man's teaching is a fountain of life
for one who would escape the snares of death.

15 Good intelligence wins favour,
but treachery leads to disaster.[b]

16 A clever man is wise and conceals everything,
but the stupid parade their folly.

17 An evil messenger causes trouble,[c]
but a trusty envoy makes all go well again.

18 To refuse correction brings poverty and contempt;
one who takes a reproof to heart comes to honour.

19 Lust indulged sickens a man;[d]
stupid people loathe to mend their ways.

20 Walk with the wise and be wise;
mix with the stupid and be misled.

21 Ill fortune follows the sinner close behind,
but good rewards the righteous.

22 A good man leaves an inheritance to his descendants,
but the sinner's hoard passes to the righteous.

[a] quickly come by: *so Sept.; Heb.* because of emptiness.
[b] leads to disaster: *prob. rdg., cp. Sept.; Heb.* is enduring.
[c] causes trouble: *or* is unsuccessful.
[d] Lust...a man: *or* Desire fulfilled is pleasant to the appetite.

Untilled land might yield food enough for the poor,   23
but even that may be lost through injustice.
A father who spares the rod hates his son,   24
but one who loves him keeps him in order.
A righteous man eats his fill,   25
    but the wicked go hungry.

☆ 1. *sees the reason for*: this phrase is missing in the Hebrew.
A word has to be supplied; and 'accepts' would meet the
case equally well. The *arrogant man*, who has already been
mentioned in 3: 34 and in 9: 7–8 (where the Hebrew word is
translated 'insolent'), is unteachable because he is sure that he
knows best. The ideal pupil is the one who meekly accepts his
father's – or teacher's – *correction*: answering back was not
encouraged.

3. *minds his words*: literally, 'guards his mouth'. The person
who does not think before he speaks is bound eventually to
blurt out something which will give serious offence. Compare
Amen-em-opet III 5: 13: 'Sleep a night before speaking.'

6. *To do right is the protection of*: literally, 'righteousness
protects'. 'Righteousness' and 'wickedness' are regarded
almost in a personal way. They stand for conformity to the
Order and rebellion against it, and their consequences follow
naturally without the need for a special divine intervention.
This type of saying should be distinguished from sayings like
12: 2, where the consequences of human conduct are attributed to divine intervention; but neither type is restricted to
Israelite wisdom literature.

7–8. Two sayings on *wealth*.

7. As the footnote shows, there are two possible ways of interpreting this saying. It may be simply a comment on the
perverseness of human nature, or, like 15: 16 and 19: 1,
it may mean that true wealth does not consist in worldly
goods.

8. The interpretation of the Hebrew here is uncertain; if

the N.E.B. translation is correct it means that riches have their disadvantages, and that the *poor man* is at least free from the likelihood of being kidnapped and held to ransom.

9. *embers*: literally, 'lamp'. 'Light' and 'lamp' symbolize life, that is, happiness and prosperity. The metaphor of the lamp may have been derived from the ever-burning lamp in the temple at Jerusalem which symbolized the presence of God with his people. Here it is applied to the individual.

10. *friends in council*: if the text is correct the point is that two heads are better than one, and that it is only the fool who is sure that he knows best. But the second line of the verse is exactly identical with 11: 26 except that the letters of the word translated 'friends in council' in 13: 10 are in a different order in 11: 26, giving a word which means 'modest persons'. If this was the original text here also there would be a better antithesis, between presumption and modesty.

11. Like the English saying 'Easy come, easy go', this is the kind of sentiment with which the man of modest means and no expectations comforts himself. There is no suggestion that the *wealth quickly come by* has been gained dishonestly: the moral, if there is one, is simply that there is nothing to beat hard work. Compare this saying, however, with 28: 20, where it seems to be implied that it is impossible to make a quick fortune honestly.

12. This is simply an observation on human psychology. The *heart* (see the note on 4: 23) was the seat of the will: consequently *makes the heart sick* means 'saps a man's vital energy'.

a staff of life: the Hebrew expression is the same as that which the N.E.B. has rendered in 3: 18 by 'staff of life' but in 11: 30 by 'tree of life'. In the present context there is little to show which is the more appropriate translation.

13–14. Two sayings about the importance of paying attention to wise *advice*.

14. *a fountain of life*: see the note on 10: 11.

the snares of death: behind this expression lies the mythological concept of the god Death as a hunter, laying snares. See the note on 1: 12.

15. It is difficult to see any close relationship between the two lines of this saying.

16. In the N.E.B. translation this verse is identical in meaning with 12: 23. But the word translated *conceals* does not usually have this meaning. A more conventional translation of the line would be 'In everything the prudent man acts with knowledge' – that is, he does not act until he has studied the facts.

17. The function of ambassador was among those for which the wisdom schools prepared their pupils: in the Prologue to *Amen-em-opet* it is stated that one of the aims of the book is to enable the pupil 'to return a report to one who has sent him' (1: 6). This saying therefore perhaps points to a particular social class, although it is possible that envoys or middlemen may also have been employed for less exalted commercial or social purposes within Israel itself. Such men would be subject to the temptation to falsify the messages with which they were entrusted for their own private gain, with disastrous consequences for their employers.

19. It is difficult to see any connection between the two lines of this saying. If the correct rendering of the first line is that given by the N.E.B. footnote, i.e. 'Desire fulfilled is pleasant to the appetite', the sentiment expressed is similar to that of verse 12 *b*; indeed, it would form an excellent counterpart to verse 12 *a*.

20. The force of this saying depended on the sounds of the words in Hebrew: the words translated *mix* and *misled* are quite different verbs, but have similar sounds. We may compare the word-play in the saying 'A friend in need is a friend indeed'.

21–2. Two sayings contrasting the fates of the *good man* and the *sinner*.

22. Whereas verse 21 states the principle of retribution in absolute terms, this verse appears to recognize an exception to it. Even though ill fortune usually dogs the sinner, there are

cases where the sinner dies rich. But the principle of a just reward is still maintained: eventually the ill-gotten gains will pass to the righteous, and so the amassing of them will find its justification.

23. The first line of this verse is difficult, and the N.E.B. translation is conjectural.

24. Corporal punishment was regarded as an essential element in children's education. Compare the following quotations from texts which Egyptian schoolboys were required to learn and copy out: 'Boys have their ears on their backsides: they listen when they are beaten'; and (a testimony from a former pupil!): 'You caned me, and so your teaching entered my ear.' The point of this saying is that spoiling a child is a sign, not of parental love, but of the lack of it. ✲

14 The wisest women build up their homes;
the foolish pull them down with their own hands.

2   A straightforward man fears the LORD;
the double-dealer scorns him.

3   The speech of a fool is a rod for his back;[a]
a wise man's words are his safeguard.

4   Where there are no oxen the barn is empty,
but the strength of a great ox ensures rich crops.

5   A truthful witness is no liar;
a false witness tells a pack of lies.

6   A conceited man seeks wisdom, yet finds none;
to one of understanding, knowledge comes easily.

7   Avoid a stupid man,
you will hear not a word of sense from him.

8   A clever man has the wit to find the right way;
the folly of stupid men misleads them.

9   A fool is too arrogant to make amends;
upright men know what reconciliation means.

[a] his back: *prob. rdg.; Heb.* pride.

The heart knows its own bitterness,   10
and a stranger has no part in its joy.
The house of the wicked will be torn down,   11
but the home of the upright flourishes.
A road may seem straightforward to a man,   12
yet may end as the way to death.
Even in laughter the heart may grieve,   13
and mirth may end in sorrow.
The renegade reaps the fruit of his conduct,   14
a good man the fruit of his own achievements.
A simple man believes every word he hears;   15
a clever man understands the need for proof.
A wise man is cautious and turns his back on evil;   16
the stupid is heedless and falls headlong.
Impatience runs into folly;   17
distinction comes by careful thought.[a]
The simple wear the trappings of folly;   18
the clever are crowned with knowledge.
Evil men cringe before the good,   19
wicked men at the righteous man's door.
A poor man is odious even to his friend;   20
the rich have friends in plenty.
He who despises a hungry man[b] does wrong,   21
but he who is generous to the poor is happy.
Do not those who intend evil go astray,   22
while those with good intentions are loyal and faithful?
The pains of toil bring gain,   23
but mere talk brings nothing but poverty.
Insight is the crown of the wise;   24
folly the chief ornament of the stupid.

[a] distinction...thought: *prob. rdg.*; *Heb.* a man of careful thought is
hated.
[b] a hungry man: *so Sept.*; *Heb.* his friend.

25 A truthful witness saves life;
    the false accuser utters nothing but lies.

26 A strong man who trusts in the fear of the LORD
    will be a refuge for his sons.

27 The fear of the LORD is the fountain of life
    for the man who would escape the snares of death.

28 Many subjects make a famous king;
    with none to rule, a prince is ruined.

29 To be patient shows great understanding;
    quick temper is the height of folly.

30 A tranquil mind puts flesh on a man,
    but passion rots his bones.

31 He who oppresses*a* the poor insults his Maker;
    he who is generous to the needy honours him.

32 An evil man is brought down by his wickedness;
    the upright man is secure in his own honesty.*b*

33 Wisdom is at home in a discerning mind,
    but is ill at ease in the heart of a fool.

34 Righteousness raises a people to honour;
    to do wrong is a disgrace to any nation.

35 A king shows favour to an intelligent servant,
    but his displeasure strikes down those who fail him.

---

* 1. *The wisest women*: the objection to this translation is that
the verb is in the singular: the N.E.B. translators have taken
this to be a mistake for the plural. But there is another possible
solution: if the word *women* is omitted as a later addition based
on a misunderstanding, the line becomes almost identical with
9: 1 *a*: 'Wisdom has built her house'. This provides a parallelism with the next line, where the Hebrew has, not *the
foolish*, but 'folly'. The saying could then be regarded as a
briefer statement of the point which is made in the contrast

[*a*] Or slanders.   [*b*] honesty: *so Sept.*; Heb. death.

82

between Wisdom and the woman of foolishness in 9: 1–6, 13–18.

4. *the barn is empty*: the Hebrew here is obscure. The N.E.B. translation makes this line simply a negative equivalent of the next line. The Hebrew seems to mean 'a mangerful of grain', which is almost the opposite. If that is the correct interpretation the point may be that the farmer has to balance the grain consumption of the ox with the value of the work which it does; and if he does so he will realize that it is well worth the expense.

5. See the note on 12: 17. The second line is identical with the first line of 6: 19.

9. The whole of this verse is difficult. The N.E.B. translation represents only one of the possible guesses at its meaning.

10. This saying recognizes that the individual human personality has depth impenetrable to the outsider, and displays a high degree of individual self-consciousness.

12–13. Two sayings about false appearances.

12. Here again the *road* or way is a symbol of human behaviour. The expression *the way to death* recalls the warnings in chapters 1–9 against the 'ways' of the adulterous woman, but the point here is somewhat different: it refers to the difficulty which we frequently experience in making moral decisions.

15–17. Three sayings on the need for caution.

15. *understands the need for proof*: alternatively, 'watches his step'.

17. *distinction*: that is, a high place in society. The Hebrew reads 'the man of careful thought is hated', but this makes no sense. The N.E.B. translation is based on a slight alteration of the text. Patience and self-control are among the chief characteristics of the ideal man in ancient Near Eastern wisdom literature.

18. In the N.E.B. translation it is difficult to see what the point of this saying is. The usual translation of the verb which

the N.E.B. renders *wear the trappings of* is 'inherit' or 'acquire'. This would give more point to the saying: there is a contrast, as in verse 15, between the *simple* man (see the note on 1:22) who has not yet received the benefit of education, and the *clever* man who has. The simple, uninstructed man will finish up as an unredeemable fool, doomed to disgrace; but the man who has been taught how to use his judgement will end up *crowned with knowledge*, that is, respected by all for his wisdom.

20. No moral is implied here. It is a simple observation that no one wants to know the poor man.

21. *a hungry man*: the N.E.B. has followed the Septuagint rather than the Hebrew, which has 'his neighbour'. This makes a better parallelism; but the Hebrew makes sense and may be right.

22. If the N.E.B. interpretation is correct, this is an example (compare 12:17) of those sayings whose form makes them into statements of the obvious, but whose intention is to urge the reader to avoid evil behaviour. But there is another way of taking it: *go astray* may refer to the unpleasant fate of the wicked rather than to their deeds, and similarly in the second line, instead of *are loyal and faithful*, we ought perhaps to translate 'meet with loyalty and faithfulness': that is, the good also receive their due reward in making many loyal friends.

24. *Insight*: if this is the correct translation this saying presumably means that a man's wisdom or folly cannot be hidden, but shows itself in his actions. But the word could also be translated 'wealth', which gives it rather more point: wisdom brings success in life, but the only reward of the stupid man is his own lamentable folly.

25. The first line of this saying is to be taken literally: by giving true testimony in court a witness may save the life of an innocent defendant. The second line is a variant of the second lines of 12:17; 14:5.

26–7. Two sayings about *the fear of the LORD*.

26. The first line of this saying could also be rendered 'In the fear of the LORD is a strong man's confidence'; the second

line would then begin 'and it will be...'. On the *fear of the LORD* see the note on 1: 7.

a refuge: presumably from the dangers which are the consequence of irreligion.

27. On the relationship between this verse and 13: 14 see p. 59.

snares of death: see the note on 13: 14.

28. The rebellions against David (2 Sam. 15–20) illustrate the point of this saying.

29–30. Two psychological sayings.

29. Here again we have the ideal of self-control which is common to all ancient Near Eastern wisdom literature.

30. This observation, which is in line with modern medical opinion, is also found in Egyptian wisdom literature, especially in *Amen-em-opet* IV, which contrasts the fates of the 'hothead' and the 'truly silent man' – that is, the self-controlled man.

31. The duty of kindness to the *poor* is recognized in the ethical codes of many peoples including those of the ancient Near East; but the motive given here, which is also found in 17: 5 and Job 31: 15, seems to be an original contribution of Israelite wisdom literature. It is often said to be due to the influence of the prophets, but this is doubtful: only Mal. 2: 10 comes anywhere near it, and even then it is in the narrow context of Jewish social relationships. It is characteristic of Jewish wisdom literature that it took the doctrine of creation very seriously as a theological concept. Jesus in his teaching (Matt. 25: 31–46) takes the idea further still: 'Anything you did for one of my brothers here, however humble, you did for me' (verse 40).

34. Here the wisdom teacher applies the principles of individual behaviour to national policy. It may be that the influence of prophets such as Isaiah on national policy (see pp. 9–10) can be seen here.

35. *servant*: the Hebrew word was used of all officials from the highest to the lowest. *

15   A soft answer turns away anger,
      but a sharp word makes tempers hot.

2   A wise man's tongue spreads knowledge;
      stupid men talk nonsense.

3   The eyes of the LORD are everywhere,
      surveying evil and good men alike.

4   A soothing word is a staff of life,
      but a mischievous tongue breaks the spirit.

5   A fool spurns his father's correction,
      but to take a reproof to heart shows good sense.

6   In the righteous man's house there is ample wealth;
      the gains of the wicked bring trouble.

7   The lips of a wise man promote knowledge;
      the hearts of the stupid are dishonest.

8   The wicked man's sacrifice is abominable to the LORD;
      the good man's prayer is his delight.

9   The conduct of the wicked is abominable to the LORD,
      but he loves the seeker after righteousness.

10   A man who leaves the main road resents correction,
      and he who hates reproof will die.

11   Sheol and Abaddon lie open before the LORD,
      how much more the hearts of men!

12   The conceited man does not take kindly to reproof
      and he will not consult the wise.

13   A merry heart makes a cheerful face;
      heartache crushes the spirit.

14   A discerning mind seeks knowledge,
      but the stupid man feeds on folly.

15   In the life of the downtrodden every day is wretched,
      but to have a glad heart is a perpetual feast.

16   Better a pittance with the fear of the LORD
      than great treasure and trouble in its train.

17   Better a dish of vegetables if love go with it

than a fat ox eaten in hatred.

Bad temper provokes a quarrel, 18
but patience heals discords.

The path of the sluggard is a tangle of weeds, 19
but the road of the diligent*a* is a highway.

A wise son brings joy to his father; 20
a young fool despises his mother.

Folly may amuse the empty-headed; 21
a man of understanding makes straight for his goal.

Schemes lightly made come to nothing, 22
but with long planning they succeed.

A man may be pleased with his own retort; 23
how much better is a word in season!

For men of intelligence the path of life leads upwards 24
and keeps them clear of Sheol below.

The LORD pulls down the proud man's home 25
but fixes the widow's boundary-stones.

A bad man's thoughts are the LORD's abomination, 26
but the words of the pure are a delight.*b*

A grasping man brings trouble on his family, 27
but he who spurns a bribe will enjoy long life.

The righteous think before they answer; 28
a bad man's ready tongue is full of mischief.

The LORD stands aloof from the wicked, 29
he listens to the righteous man's prayer.

A bright look brings joy to the heart, 30
and good news warms a man's marrow.

Whoever listens to wholesome reproof 31
shall enjoy the society of the wise.

He who refuses correction is his own worst enemy, 32
but he who listens to reproof learns sense.

[a] *So Sept.; Heb.* the upright.
[b] the words...delight: *or* gracious words are pure.

33   The fear of the LORD is a training in wisdom,
     and the way to honour is humility.

✻ 1. *A soft answer*: not an obsequious answer, but one which 'takes the steam out' of a situation and makes calm discussion possible. Such statesmanlike speech was regarded by the authors of the Egyptian Instructions as an essential qualification of the courtier.

3. The idea that God sees all and that nothing can be hidden from him is not confined to the wisdom literature; but its formulation here is reminiscent of the statement in *Amen-em-opet* XV 17: 9–12 that the eye of the moon-god 'travels round the Two Lands (that is, Egypt)', observing and punishing misdeeds.

4. *staff of life*: or, 'tree of life'. See the note on 13: 12.

8–9. Two sayings about conduct which is *abominable to the LORD*. See the note on 3: 32.

8. There is no condemnation of *sacrifice* as such here. It is the insincere and therefore blasphemous sacrifice of the *wicked man* which is condemned. This teaching is similar to that of some of the prophets (e.g. Isa. 1: 10–17; Amos 5: 21–4), but is much more ancient, occurring in the early Egyptian *Instruction for King Merikare*: 'More acceptable (to God) is the character of the righteous man than the (sacrificial) ox of the evildoer.'

the good man's prayer: the point is not that prayer is more efficacious than sacrifice, but on the contrary that it may normally be expected to be less so. Sacrifice is regarded here as a gift to God which accompanies prayer; and the point is that the good man, even if his prayer is not accompanied by such a gift, will receive God's favour whereas the wicked man's expensive sacrifice will be repugnant to him.

10. *the main road*: see the note on 4: 10–19.

resents correction: an alternative translation would be 'must suffer correction'.

will die: not in the sense of eternal death. The meaning is that the man will die before his time.

11. *Sheol and Abaddon*: both these words refer to the place beneath the earth to which men go when they die. In the Old Testament there are passages which suggest that the dead are beyond even God's reach. This saying assumes that God is fully cognizant of what goes on in Sheol. The idea is similar to that of verse 3.

12. *the wise*: it is often assumed that this refers to professional wisdom teachers, but it may have a more general meaning.

13. These are simple observations of life with no moral attached; compare 14: 13, which looks at the same situation from a somewhat different angle.

14. *feeds on folly*: both knowledge and folly create an appetite for more.

15-17. A group of sayings which teach that poverty is not an absolute evil but has compensations.

15. The point of this saying seems to be that 'life is what you make it'.

16-17. There is a striking parallel to these sentiments in *Amen-em-opet* VI 9: 5-8:

> Better is poverty in God's hands
> than riches in the storehouse;
> better is plain bread when the heart is happy
> than wealth with sorrow.

20. This verse is almost identical with 10: 1.

22. This verse is very similar to 11: 14.

23. Compare the late Egyptian *Instructions of Onchsheshonqy* 12: 24: 'Do not make a statement if it is not the time for it.'

24. *upwards*: the N.E.B. translation seems to imply a doctrine of eternal life in heaven. But the Hebrew word need mean no more than 'above ground', that is, in the 'land of the living' as contrasted with the underground 'land of the dead'. Some commentators, however, believe that the words

upwards and *below* are additions made to the text in order to introduce a doctrine of eternal life and death which was not originally there. In that case the first line would originally have read 'A path of life is reserved for men of intelligence'.

25. The author of this saying is not denying that social injustice occurs, but rather asserting that it will not be allowed to go unchecked. The *proud man's home* or country estate was often acquired through the appropriation of the property of the defenceless poor. Widows were especially vulnerable to this kind of oppression, and both the laws and the wisdom literature of the ancient Near East frequently condemn the crime of moving or removing *boundary-stones*, which constituted legal proof of ownership. It was believed that this was a matter with which God particularly concerned himself: for example, in *Amen-em-opet* VI 8: 12, where this crime is condemned, it is stated that God 'fixes the boundaries of the arable land'. The Israelite prophets also warned that God would not permit such crimes to go unpunished but would bring about the ruin of those guilty of them: compare, for example, Isa. 5: 8–10:

> Shame on you! you who add house to house
>> and join field to field,
>> until not an acre remains,
> and you are left to dwell alone in the land.
>> The LORD of Hosts has sworn in my hearing;
>> Many houses shall go to ruin,
>> fine large houses shall be uninhabited.
>> Five acres of vineyard shall yield only a gallon,
>> and ten bushels of seed return only a peck.

27. Bribery also is universally condemned in the literature of the ancient Near East. See the note on 17: 8 on the apparent inconsistency of Proverbs on this subject.

30. *A bright look*: the meaning of the phrase so translated is not certain.

31–3. Three sayings about the importance of paying attention to wise teachers.

31. See the note on verse 12.

33. This saying belongs to the latest material in the book, in which the *training in wisdom* offered by the wisdom teacher has been accepted as fully in accordance with the *fear of the LORD*, that is, the religion of Israel. ✶

A man may order his thoughts,   **16**
but the LORD inspires the words he utters.
A man's whole conduct may be pure in his own eyes, 2
but the LORD fixes a standard for the spirit of man.
Commit to the LORD all that you do,   3
and your plans will be fulfilled.
The LORD has made each thing for its own end;   4
he made even the wicked for a day of disaster.
Proud men, one and all, are abominable to the LORD; 5
depend upon it:*a* they will not escape punishment.
Guilt is wiped out by faith and loyalty,   6
and the fear of the LORD makes men turn from evil.
When the LORD is pleased with a man and his ways, 7
he makes even his enemies live at peace with him.
Better a pittance honestly earned   8
than great gains ill gotten.
Man plans his journey by his own wit,   9
but it is the LORD who guides his steps.
The king's mouth is an oracle,   10
he cannot err when he passes sentence.
Scales*b* and balances*c* are the LORD's concern;   11
all the weights in the bag are his business.
Wickedness is abhorrent to kings,   12

[a] depend upon it: *lit.* hand on hand.
[b] *Or* Pointer.
[c] *Prob. rdg.; Heb.* balances of justice.

for a throne rests firm on righteousness.

13 Honest speech is the desire of kings,
they love a man who speaks the truth.

14 A king's anger is a messenger of death,
and a wise man will appease it.

15 In the light of the king's countenance is life,
his favour is like a rain-cloud in the spring.

16 How much better than gold it is to gain wisdom,
and to gain discernment is better than pure silver.[a]

17 To turn from evil is the highway of the upright;
watch your step and save your life.

18 Pride comes before disaster,
and arrogance before a fall.

19 Better sit humbly with those in need
than divide the spoil with the proud.

20 The shrewd man of business will succeed well,
but the happy man is he who trusts in the LORD.

21 The sensible man seeks advice from the wise,
he drinks it in and increases his knowledge.[b]

22 Intelligence is a fountain of life to its possessors,
but a fool is punished by his own folly.

23 The wise man's mind guides his speech,
and what his lips impart increases learning.[c]

24 Kind words are like dripping honey,
sweetness on the tongue and health for the body.

25 A road may seem straightforward to a man,
yet may end as the way to death.

26 The labourer's appetite is always plaguing him,
his hunger spurs him on.

[a] better than pure silver: *so Targ.; Heb.* choicer than silver.
[b] he drinks...knowledge: *or* and he whose speech is persuasive increases learning.
[c] and what...learning: *or* and increases the learning of his utterance.

A scoundrel repeats evil gossip;　27
it is like a scorching fire on his lips.
Disaffection stirs up quarrels,　28
and tale-bearing breaks up friendship.
A man of violence draws others on　29
and leads them into lawless ways.
The man who narrows his eyes is disaffected at heart,　30
and a close-lipped man is bent on mischief.
Grey hair is a crown of glory,　31
and it is won by a virtuous life.
Better be slow to anger than a fighter,　32
better govern one's temper than capture a city.
The lots may be cast into the lap,　33
but the issue depends wholly on the LORD.

✳ This chapter shows clearer signs of arrangement by subject than most. Verses 1–9, except verse 8, are concerned with God's control of human life, and verses 10–15, except verse 11, are about kings. There are also other traces of such attempts at classification.

　1. *but the LORD inspires the words he utters*: literally, 'from Yahweh is the answer of the tongue'. God overrules men's plans when they are not in accordance with his will. Compare *Papyrus Insinger* XXIV 31: 11: 'God directs the heart and tongue of man as he pleases.'

　2. *fixes a standard for the spirit of man*: alternatively, 'gauges men's spirits'. The latter interpretation has some resemblance to the Egyptian belief that a man's heart was weighed in the balance after death to ascertain whether in life it had conformed to 'truth'.

　3. Compare verse 1.

　4. This saying asserts that every created thing fits into a pattern or Order: *the wicked* were created so that they might suffer the fate which was appropriate for them. This rather curious argument may have been prompted by the question

'Why did God create the wicked?'. If so, it may be the first hint of the more serious questioning of God's justice which we find in such books as Job.

5. *abominable to the LORD*: see the note on 3: 32.

depend upon it: see the note on 11: 21.

6. *is wiped out*: this verb, elsewhere translated in the N.E.B. by 'make expiation', is primarily used in the Old Testament to denote the removal of sin through sacrifice. Here this is achieved not through sacrifice but by repentance: by a return to *faith and loyalty*, that is, to the standards of conduct characteristic of the relationship between Yahweh and Israel. This is put in another way in the second line: a man can be saved from the consequences of his evil deeds if the *fear of the LORD*, that is, his knowledge of what is due to God, still retains some power over him: reflection on this will enable him to *turn from evil* and so regain God's favour. This saying has no parallels in non-Israelite wisdom literature but expresses an Israelite point of view found also in the prophets and Psalms.

7. *his enemies*: that is, personal enemies. The meaning is that the man who has God's favour has no enemies: this is the way in which God rewards him.

8. The point of this saying is different from that of 15: 16, although the wording is partly the same. Here the theme is not wealth as such but the way in which it is acquired. Compare *Amen-em-opet* VI 8: 19–20:

> Better is a single measure given by God
> than five thousand taken illegally.

9. Compare verse 1.

10, 12–15. These sayings are all about *kings*, but otherwise have nothing in common. They would have been of interest mainly to courtiers, who came into regular contact with the king.

10. The belief that kings possessed divinely given powers of judgement was common to all the ancient Near Eastern

peoples, including Israel, although some passages, especially in the prophets, show that it was questioned in some circles. For examples of the reputation of Israelite kings as unerring judges compare the judgement of Solomon (1 Kings 3: 16–28) and the wise woman's comment to David in 2 Sam. 14: 20: 'Your majesty is as wise as the angel of God and knows all that goes on in the land.'

11. See the note on 11: 1.

12. *Wickedness...righteousness*: probably these words refer to the subjects of the king rather than to the king himself.

abhorrent to kings: the word translated 'abhorrent' is the same as that translated 'abominable' in the phrase 'abominable to the LORD' elsewhere (e.g. verse 5).

14. Although Israelite kings were not above the law, they had executive powers of life and death in practice. The phrase *a messenger of death* is aptly illustrated by Solomon's political assassinations of Adonijah, Joab and Shimei (1 Kings 2: 25, 29–34, 46).

15. The courtier is warned that his career and even his life are dependent on the king's pleasure. The use in the second line of a simile from nature probably reflects the belief that the fertility of the land depended on the well-being of the king: compare Ps. 72: 15–17.

a rain-cloud in the spring: this refers to the coming of the 'latter rains' on which the year's crop depended. As the appearance of the cloud was a harbinger of prosperity, so the favour of the king promised a successful career to the courtier.

16. This comparison was a commonplace of Old Testament wisdom. But as 3: 13–18 shows, there is no disparagement of wealth here: the man who has wisdom will have material wealth as well.

18–19. Two sayings about *arrogance*.

18. Compare *Papyrus Insinger* VII 4: 22: 'Pride and arrogance are the destruction of their master'.

19. *divide the spoil*: the term is primarily a military one, but here it probably refers to the sharing of loot by a gang of

criminals. Their 'pride' consists in their refusal to accept the rule of law.

20. In the N.E.B. translation this saying means that business acumen is a good thing, but that piety brings even better results in terms of material wealth. This thought is uncharacteristic of Proverbs. The *but* of the N.E.B. could however equally well be translated by 'and', which would make the two lines parallel rather than antithetic. But the meaning of the first line is uncertain, and the phrase translated *The shrewd man of business* perhaps means rather 'the man who is quick to take advice'.

21. The N.E.B. footnote gives an alternative translation of the second line, but does not point out that the translation of the first line is also uncertain. It ought perhaps to be translated 'The wise man will acquire a reputation for competence'.

22. *a fountain of life*: see the note on 10: 11. The second line could equally well be translated 'It is foolish to undertake the instruction of fools'.

25. This verse is identical with 14: 12.

26. *is always plaguing him*: or, 'works for him'. The point seems to be that the poor *labourer* never gets enough to eat, and that it is his hunger which drives him to work. There is a play on words here: the words translated by *labourer* and *plaguing* are similar in Hebrew, and their repetition makes a kind of jingle. No moral is drawn, and the cryptic nature of the saying may be deliberate: it is a 'hard saying' or riddle.

27–8. Two sayings about malicious *gossip* and slander.

27. *repeats evil gossip*: the meaning of the Hebrew is probably 'digs up mischief'. The point is that tales spread by irresponsible or malicious persons can be extremely damaging.

29. On the *man of violence* see further 1: 10–19.

30. These mannerisms are reminiscent of those condemned in 6: 13, but here they are probably to be understood as signs of an evil character which ought to warn others against such a person.

31. The idea behind this expression of respect for old age is

that only the righteous can attain it: the wicked are cut off before their time.

32. Military prowess then as now tended to steal the limelight from the less flamboyant virtues. This saying commends the virtues of self-control, so strongly emphasized in wisdom literature throughout the ancient Near East: it is the patient administrator who gets to the top and stays there.

33. The casting of *lots* was used in Israel at some periods as a means of discovering the will of God (e.g. 1 Sam. 14: 41–2). But this saying probably refers to the practice of casting lots without reference to God, especially to allot the shares of spoils or loot, as in Ps. 22: 18. The point is then, as in verses 1, 3 and 9, that although men think that they decide their own fate it is really God who makes the decisions. The same idea is found in *Amen-em-opet* XVIII 19: 16–17:

> One thing are the words which men say,
> another is that which God does.

Compare also *Papyrus Insinger* VII 5: 11: 'If fate and fortune come, it is God who sends them.' ✳

Better a dry crust and concord with it   **17**
than a house full of feasting and strife.
A wise slave may give orders to a disappointing son   2
and share the inheritance with the brothers.
The melting-pot is for silver and the crucible for gold, 3
but it is the LORD who assays the hearts of men.
A rogue gives a ready ear to mischievous talk,   4
and a liar listens to slander.
A man who sneers at the poor insults his Maker,   5
and he who gloats over another's ruin will answer for it.
Grandchildren are the crown of old age,   6
and sons are proud of their fathers.
Fine talk is out of place in a boor,   7
how much more is falsehood in the noble!

8 He who offers[a] a bribe finds it work like a charm,[b]
he prospers in all he undertakes.

9 He who conceals another's offence seeks his goodwill,
but he who harps on something breaks up friendship.

10 A reproof is felt by a man of discernment
more than a hundred blows by a stupid man.

11 An evil man is set only on disobedience,
but a messenger without mercy will be sent against him.

12 Better face a she-bear robbed of her cubs
than a stupid man in his folly.

13 If a man repays evil for good,
evil will never quit his house.

14 Stealing water starts a quarrel;
drop a dispute before you bare your teeth.

15 To acquit the wicked and condemn the righteous,
both are abominable in the LORD's sight.

16 What use is money in the hands of a stupid man?
Can he buy wisdom if he has no sense?

17 A friend is a loving companion at all times,
and a brother is born to share troubles.

18 A man is without sense who gives a guarantee
and surrenders himself to another as surety.

19 He who loves strife loves sin.
He who builds a lofty entrance invites thieves.

20 A crooked heart will come to no good,
and a mischievous tongue will end in disaster.

21 A stupid man is the bane of his parent,
and his father has no joy in a boorish son.

22 A merry heart makes a cheerful countenance,
but low spirits sap a man's strength.

23 A wicked man accepts a bribe under his cloak

[a] He who offers: *lit.* The owner of.
[b] *Lit.* like a stone of favour.

to pervert the course of justice.

Wisdom is never out of sight of a discerning man,   24
but a stupid man's eyes are roving everywhere.

A stupid son exasperates his father   25
and is a bitter sorrow to the mother who bore him.

Again, to punish the righteous is not good   26
and it is wrong to inflict blows on men of noble mind.

Experience uses few words;   27
discernment keeps a cool head.

Even a fool, if he holds his peace, is thought wise;   28
keep your mouth shut and show your good sense.

* 1. See the note on 16: 8.

feasting and strife: literally, 'sacrifices of strife'. As in 7: 14 the reference is to a feast held when the host has a quantity of meat in his house as a consequence of the fulfilment of a sacrificial obligation. Quarrels might arise at such feasts as much as at any other.

2. This is a particular example of the principle expressed in 12: 24. Even a *slave* can get to the top and disinherit the heir by the exercise of intelligence. There is no provision for such an occurrence in the laws of the Old Testament, though a disobedient son could be put to death (Deut. 21: 18–21), and a slave could be adopted as his heir by a man who had no sons of his own (Gen. 15: 2–3). But the story of Mephibosheth and his slave Ziba (2 Sam. 16: 1–4; 19: 24–30) shows how a clever slave could contrive to *share the inheritance* or even obtain the whole of it as the result of a judicial decision by the king.

3. God's careful testing of men's character is here compared to the assaying of gold and silver to determine their purity. Compare 16: 2.

5. See the note on 14: 31.

6. This saying reflects the great importance attached by the Israelites to the family. As to have children was a blessing and childlessness a sign of divine displeasure, so to live to see one's

grandchildren was a sign of a very special blessing, since it guaranteed the honourable survival of one's family, and so of a kind of extension of oneself, into a remote future. The second line expresses the related idea that children in turn derived their honourable status from that of their fathers.

7. *noble*: the reference is probably to high rank rather than to nobility of character. It is assumed that such persons, to whom Proverbs is perhaps primarily addressed, have a 'gentlemanly' code of conduct which rules out telling lies.

8. At first sight this saying appears to contradict the principle that the wicked come to a bad end, and in particular the condemnation of bribery in verse 23. But the word translated *bribe* simply means a gift, and in many cultures even today it is a proper and normal practice to offer a present when asking a favour. The condemnation in verse 23 is not a condemnation of this custom as such, but of secret bribes to pervert the course of justice – a very different matter.

9. *conceals another's offence*: it is not clear whether this refers to the exercise of restraint in not constantly reminding a friend of his faults, or in not telling other people about them. In any case it is a simple observation that *friendship* can only exist in an atmosphere of mutual forgiveness.

11. *a messenger without mercy*: like the 'messenger of death' in 16: 14, this is the king's messenger sent to execute the courtier found to be plotting rebellion. The consequences of disloyalty to the regime were naturally emphasized in the wisdom school attached to the court.

12. The point here is that a fool is not merely pathetic and a danger to himself but also extremely dangerous to others.

13. The doctrine of retribution is expressed here in the form 'the punishment fits the crime'.

14. *Stealing water*: it is not clear why this particular crime should have been introduced here. An alternative translation of the first line would be 'The beginning of a quarrel is (like) the seeping of water' – in other words, a quarrel should be checked before it really gets going.

15. This saying refers to dishonest judges, and is clearly addressed to people who are likely to hold such offices themselves. Such conduct is universally condemned in the laws of the Old Testament and by the prophets as well as in the other literature of the ancient Near East. On *abominable in the LORD's sight* see the note on 3: 32.

16. *buy wisdom*: it is not known whether fees were charged by wisdom teachers. But the point is that there are some people who are born fools, and that even education cannot confer wisdom on them.

17. Although some commentators have taken the view that a contrast is intended here between the functions of a *friend* and of a *brother* (*and* could equally well be translated by 'but'), the parallelism is probably synonymous. True friendship and true brotherhood are both shown in adversity.

18. See the notes on 6: 1–5. *to another*: literally, 'before another'. The phrase may refer either to the person to whom the pledge is given or the person on whose behalf it is given.

gives a guarantee: literally, 'strikes hands' – to clinch the agreement.

19. There seems to be no connection between the two halves of this verse, and the meaning of the second half is obscure. The N.E.B.'s *thieves* is an interpretation of a word which normally means 'crash' or 'ruin': thieves break in and smash things. But neither translation gives a very satisfactory sense. It has been argued that instead of *entrance* we should read 'mouth': to 'make one's mouth high' would be to speak arrogantly. But it is doubtful whether this is justifiable, and the saying remains obscure.

22. *a cheerful countenance*: alternatively, 'good health'. The sentiment is similar to that of 14: 30.

23. See the note on verse 8.

24. *are roving everywhere*: literally, 'are on the ends of the earth'. The idea that ability to concentrate is a sign of intelligence is to be expected from a schoolmaster.

26. *punish*: this verb usually means 'fine'.

men of noble mind: the word translated by 'noble' is the same as that in verse 7. It normally refers to rank rather than to nobility of character. If this is so here, the two halves of the verse are not really parallel.

27–8. Two sayings on self-control, especially in speech.

27. *a cool head*: literally, 'a cool spirit'. There is a similarity here to Egyptian thought: there the 'hothead' who comes to disaster through his lack of self-control is contrasted mainly with the 'silent man' whose characteristic is self-mastery (for example in *Amen-em-opet*), but also sometimes with the 'cool man' (for example in the *Song of Antef*). The idea appears several times in Proverbs.

28. In this and similar sayings the stress on the importance of keeping silent closely resembles the teaching of Egyptian wisdom literature from the earliest times: compare not only *Amen-em-opet*, but also *Ptah-hotep*'s 'If you are silent, it is better than the *tef-tef* plant' (an unidentified but apparently rare and valuable plant) and *Ani*'s 'Do not talk a lot. Be silent, and you will be happy.' ✳

18   The man who holds aloof seeks every pretext[a]
        to bare his teeth in scorn at competent people.

  2   The foolish have no interest in seeking to understand,
        but prefer to display their wit.

  3   When wickedness comes in, in comes contempt;
        with loss of honour comes reproach.

  4   The words of a man's mouth are a gushing torrent,
        but deep is the water in the well of wisdom.[b]

  5   It is not good to show favour to the wicked
        or to deprive the righteous of justice.

  6   When the stupid man talks, contention follows;
        his words provoke blows.

  7   The stupid man's tongue is his undoing;

[a] *So Sept.; Heb.* desire.
[b] The words...wisdom: *prob. rdg., inverting phrases.*

his lips put his life in jeopardy.

A gossip's whispers are savoury morsels,   8
gulped down into the inner man.

Again, the lazy worker is own brother   9
to the man who enjoys destruction.

The name of the LORD is a tower of strength,   10
where the righteous may run for refuge.

A rich man's wealth is his strong city,   11
a towering wall, so he supposes.

Before disaster comes, a man is proud,   12
but the way to honour is humility.

To answer a question before you have heard it out   13
is both stupid and insulting.

A man's spirit may sustain him in sickness,   14
but if the spirit is wounded, who can mend it?

Knowledge comes to the discerning mind;   15
the wise ear listens to get knowledge.

A gift opens the door to the giver   16
and gains access to the great.

In a lawsuit the first speaker seems right,   17
until another steps forward and cross-questions him.

Cast lots, and settle a quarrel,   18
and so keep litigants apart.

A reluctant brother is more unyielding than a fortress,   19
and quarrels are stubborn as the bars of a castle.

A man may live by the fruit of his tongue,   20
his lips may earn him a livelihood.

The tongue has power of life and death;   21
make friends with it and enjoy its fruits.

Find a wife, and you find a good thing;   22
so you will earn the favour of the LORD.

The poor man speaks in a tone of entreaty,   23
and the rich man gives a harsh answer.

24 Some companions are good only for idle talk,
but a friend may stick closer than a brother.

✻ 1. This is a difficult verse, but it is clear that it is a condemnation of the unsociable, or perhaps better, the anti-social man (*The man who holds aloof*). It reflects the view expressed elsewhere in Proverbs, but especially in 11: 10–11, that the lives of the individual and of the community are interdependent, so that anti-social behaviour is one of the worst of crimes.

seeks every pretext: as the N.E.B. footnote indicates, the Hebrew has 'desire', and the Septuagint text has been preferred.

bare his teeth in scorn: compare 'bare your teeth' in 17: 14. This is an unusual interpretation of a verb whose meaning is generally thought to be 'break out'.

2. *display their wit*: the verb means 'to reveal oneself', and 'express their own opinions' would be an equally good translation.

3. The meaning of this saying seems to be that the wicked are punished by the contempt of society.

4. The Hebrew appears to say in the second line that a *well of wisdom* is a *gushing torrent*, and the N.E.B. translators, in order to avoid the incongruity of such a statement, have reversed the position of the last half of each line (see the footnote), supposing them to have accidentally been inverted at some stage in the transmission of the text. It is however possible to translate the Hebrew as it stands in a different way: 'The words of men are deep water, a gushing torrent and a well of wisdom.' The meaning would then be that human speech can be put to a variety of uses.

5. The wisdom teacher's statement is the equivalent of the 'Thou shalt not...' of the Old Testament laws condemning partiality in the lawcourts.

6–7. Two more sayings about stupid talk. It injures both the speaker and society in general.

8. The point of this saying is that slander is all the more

dangerous because of the flaw in human character which ensures that it is avidly listened to and remembered. The idea of
the belly or *inner man* as the seat of the memory is also found
in *Amen-em-opet*, whose author urges his reader that his
words should 'rest in the casket of your belly, that they may
be a key in your heart' (13: 13–14).

10–11. These two sayings offer two different ideas about
the way to obtain security in life: trust in God and the acqui-
sition of material wealth. Since wealth was held to be itself
a gift of God, we should probably regard them as intended to
bring out two sides of the truth rather than as being in direct
contradiction one with the other.

10. *The name of the LORD*: this is the only occurrence of this
phrase in Proverbs, but it occurs frequently elsewhere in the
Old Testament. It is almost equivalent in meaning to 'the
LORD', but often refers to some particular aspect of his nature,
here his power to protect.

11. The first line of this saying is identical with the first line
of 10: 15.

so he supposes: the meaning of this word is uncertain. The
N.E.B. translation seems to imply that the rich man is wrong
to rely on his wealth, but it is not certain that this is what is
meant.

14. Compare 14: 30; 17: 22.

16. See the note on 17: 8.

17–19. Three sayings on *quarrels* and lawsuits.

17. In Israelite legal practice the plaintiff or prosecutor
spoke first, followed by the defendant. This saying is capable
of a number of interpretations, and is probably intended to be
applied beyond its legal setting. It may be a comment on the
human propensity to be satisfied by an eloquent presentation of
one side of a story without realizing that there are usually
two sides.

18. See the note on 16: 33. There are no other examples in
the Old Testament of the use of the lot in precisely these circumstances; it may have been done when there seemed to be

no other way of settling a dispute. In such a case it would be regarded as an appeal to God for a decision. *litigants* is a translation based on a slight alteration of the text, which reads 'powerful men'.

19. The text of this verse is very difficult. The meaning of the word translated *reluctant* is uncertain; the translation *unyielding* has been obtained through an alteration of the text; and the general statement in the second line does not seem to be very closely related to the first. 'Aggrieved' would be a possible alternative to *reluctant*, and this would give somewhat better sense: quarrels between brothers are the most difficult to heal.

20–1. Two sayings on the power of speech.

20. It is unlikely that this saying refers to particular professions. The meaning is probably the same as in 12: 14: the man who uses his gift of speech for promoting harmony rather than dissension will be rewarded with prosperity. There is no specific reference to *a livelihood* in the Hebrew.

22. *Find a wife*: clearly a good wife must be meant, such as is described in 31: 10–31. The authors of Proverbs were well aware of the existence of the other kind – compare, for example, 12: 4. The epigrammatic form of the first line (only four words: 'find wife – find good') suggests that this may have been a popular saying, to which the pious second line was subsequently added.

earn the favour of the LORD: the Hebrew (literally, 'receive favour from the LORD') says nothing about earning. It is left to the interpreter to guess what is the relationship between the two lines; but the second line probably means that finding a good wife is a sign or result of God's favour, rather than its cause.

23. This saying simply states a fact of life and leaves the reader to draw a moral. There is acute observation and concise expression here: a nineteenth-century novelist such as Dickens would have taken a whole chapter to get this effect.   ✳

Better be poor and above reproach **19**
than rich and crooked in speech.
Again, desire without knowledge is not good;   2
the man in a hurry misses the way.
A man's own folly wrecks his life,   3
and then he bears a grudge against the LORD.
Wealth makes many friends,   4
but a man without means loses the friend he has.
A false witness will not escape punishment,   5
and one who utters nothing but lies will not go free.
Many curry favour with the great;   6
a lavish giver has the world for his friend.
A poor man's brothers all dislike him,   7
how much more is he shunned by his friends!
Practice in evil makes the perfect scoundrel;[a]
the man who talks too much meets his deserts.[b]
To learn sense is true self-love;   8
cherish discernment and make sure of success.
A false witness will not escape punishment,   9
and one who utters nothing but lies will perish.
A fool at the helm is out of place,   10
how much worse a slave in command of men of rank!
To be patient shows intelligence;   11
to overlook faults is a man's glory.
A king's rage is like a lion's roar,   12
his favour like dew on the grass.
A stupid son is a calamity to his father;   13
a nagging wife is like water dripping endlessly.
Home and wealth may come down from ancestors,   14
but an intelligent wife is a gift from the LORD.
Laziness is the undoing of the worthless;   15

[a] Practice...scoundrel: *so Sept.; Heb. om.*
[b] meets his deserts: *prob. rdg., cp. Sept.; Heb.* not they.

idlers must starve.

16 To keep the commandments keeps a man safe,
but scorning the way of the LORD brings death.

17 He who is generous to the poor lends to the LORD;
he will repay him in full measure.

18 Chastise your son while there is hope for him,
but be careful not to flog him to death.

19 A man's ill temper brings its own punishment;
try to save him, and you make matters worse.

20 Listen to advice and accept instruction,
and you will die a wise man.

21 A man's heart may be full of schemes,
but the LORD's purpose will prevail.

22 Greed is a disgrace to a man;
better be a poor man than a liar.

23 The fear of the LORD is life;
he who is full of it will rest untouched by evil.

24 The sluggard plunges his hand in the dish
but will not so much as lift it to his mouth.

25 Strike an arrogant man, and he resents it like a fool;
reprove an understanding man, and he understands
what you mean.

26 He who talks his father down vexes his mother;
he is a son to bring shame and disgrace on them.

27 A son[a] who ceases to accept correction
is sure to turn his back on the teachings of knowledge.

28 A rascally witness perverts justice,
and the talk of the wicked fosters mischief.

29 There is a rod[b] in pickle for the arrogant,
and blows ready for the stupid man's back.

[a] *So Sept.; Heb.* My son.
[b] *So Sept.; Heb.* judgement.

✱ 1. *rich*: the Hebrew has 'a fool'. The N.E.B. has followed the ancient Syriac translation as making better sense.

5. This verse is almost identical with verse 9, and similar to 6: 19; 14: 5, 25.

6–7 a. Two observations on the consequences of wealth and influence and the lack of them. Each reader is free, if he chooses, to draw his own moral.

7. The first two lines of this verse clearly form a complete saying. As the N.E.B. footnote points out, the third line is not found in the Hebrew, so that the final line hangs in the air, quite unrelated to the rest of the verse. The N.E.B. translators have assumed that originally there was another line to go with it, forming a separate saying, and have supplied this from the Septuagint. The last line is also difficult in the Hebrew, and the Septuagint has again provided the idea for a slight alteration of the text. But there is no certainty about this: the N.E.B. has done its best with an otherwise unintelligible text.

9. See the note on verse 5.

10. A more usual translation of the first line of this saying would be 'Luxury is out of place for a fool'. The N.E.B. translation makes better sense, though its correctness is by no means certain. If 'luxury' is the correct translation the two halves of the saying seem to have little relationship to one another, unless it is that each draws attention to something which is incongruous, like 17: 7. Lists of incongruous things may have had their place in wisdom literature as part of the process of classifying similar phenomena: there is another in Ecclus. 25: 2, which lists 'a poor man who boasts, a rich man who lies, and an old fool who commits adultery'.

a slave in command: compare 12: 24; 17: 2. We must assume that such a thing was a real possibility in Israelite society.

12. See the notes on 16: 14, 15.

13. Both halves of this verse express sentiments found elsewhere in this section. The second line with its wry humour is evidently a cry from the heart!

14. This saying was probably placed here because of the contrast of the second line with the second line of the previous verse. The point is not quite the same as that of 18:22: the phrase *a gift from the LORD* is used here to suggest that in contrast to the other, predictable, circumstances of a man's life, marriage is liable to contain an element of the unexpected.

15. *the worthless*: this word is usually translated by 'sleep' or 'lethargy': 'Laziness produces lethargy' would therefore be an alternative translation of the first line.

16. *the way of the LORD*: there is no reference at all to God in the Hebrew, which has 'he who despises his ways will die'. 'Despising one's ways' probably means not paying sufficient regard to one's conduct. *commandments* in the first line then probably refers to the teaching of the wisdom teacher or the father, as elsewhere in Proverbs. But if the emendation preferred by the N.E.B. is correct, the saying is a warning that happiness is to be found only in obedience to God.

17. Compare 14:31. The idea is hardly disinterested; but the belief that all good conduct would receive its proper reward was so ingrained that it could hardly be expected to be absent from the mind even of the generous man. Here the reward is to be received in this life; but even in the New Testament the 'reward in heaven' plays an important role in the teaching of Jesus, and Peter's enquiry what reward the disciples are to get for following Jesus (Matt. 19:27) receives not a rebuke but a positive assurance.

18. On corporal punishment see the note on 23:13–14.

be careful not to flog him to death: an alternative translation would be 'and do not contrive to bring about his death', meaning that to refrain from applying the rod would result in the boy's growing up wicked or stupid and so inevitably incurring death as a result of his behaviour. The thought would then be the same as that of 23:13–14.

19. *you make matters worse*: or, 'you will have to do it again and again'.

20. *die a wise man*: or, 'end by being a wise man'.

21. For comparable sayings in Egyptian wisdom literature see the note on 16: 33.

22. The Hebrew of the first line reads 'A man's desire is his loyalty'. Since this appears to make no sense, most commentators have tried to solve the problem by assuming that either 'desire' or 'loyalty' is a mistake. The N.E.B. has taken the latter course, assuming that instead of 'loyalty' the original text has a word meaning 'disgrace'. The problem is unsolved; the N.E.B. translation makes a fairly good parallel with the second line.

23. Here again the second line is difficult, but its meaning is probably parallel to that of the first.

24. A humorous vignette of the man so lazy that he cannot even get through the process of eating. This saying is clearly intended to be applied more widely against those who start an activity but lack the energy to carry it through.

25. The word translated *resents* normally means 'be sensible'. The second half of the first line could therefore be rendered 'and a simple person will learn sense': that is, he will take warning from the punishment suffered by the arrogant man. The meaning would then be the same as in 21: 11. ✶

Wine is an insolent fellow, and strong drink makes an **20**
    uproar;
  no one addicted to their company grows wise.
A king's threat is like a lion's roar;   2
  one who ignores it is his own worst enemy.
To draw back from a dispute is honourable;   3
  it is the fool who bares his teeth.
The sluggard who does not plough in autumn   4
  goes begging at harvest and gets nothing.
Counsel in another's heart is like deep water,   5
  but a discerning man will draw it up.
Many a man protests his loyalty,   6
  but where will you find one to keep faith?

7 If a man leads a good and upright life,
  happy are the sons who come after him!

8 A king seated on the judgement-throne
  has an eye to sift all that is evil.

9 Who can say, 'I have a clear conscience;
  I am purged from my sin'?

10 A double standard in weights and measures
   is an abomination to the LORD.

11 Again, a young man is known by his actions,
   whether his conduct is innocent or guilty.*

12 The ear that hears, the eye that sees,
   the LORD made them both.

13 Love sleep, and you will end in poverty;
   keep your eyes open, and you will eat your fill.

14 'A bad bargain!' says the buyer to the seller,
   but off he goes to brag about it.

15 There is gold in plenty and coral too,
   but a wise word is a rare jewel.

16 Take a man's garment when he pledges his word for a
        stranger
   and hold that as a pledge for the unknown person.

17 Bread got by fraud tastes good,
   but afterwards it fills the mouth with grit.

18 Care is the secret of good planning;
   wars are won by skilful strategy.

19 A gossip will betray secrets;*
   have nothing to do with a tattler.

20 If a man reviles father and mother,
   his lamp will go out when darkness comes.

21 If you begin by piling up property in haste,*

[a] *Prob. rdg.; Heb.* upright.
[b] *Or* He who betrays secrets is a gossip.
[c] by...haste: *or, as otherwise read,* by wrongfully withholding an inheritance.

it will bring you no blessing in the end.

Do not think to repay evil for evil,   22
wait for the LORD to deliver you.

A double standard in weights is an abomination to the 23
 LORD,
and false scales are not good in his sight.[a]

It is the LORD who directs a man's steps;   24
how can mortal man understand the road he travels?

It is dangerous to dedicate a gift rashly   25
or to make a vow and have second thoughts.

A wise king sifts out the wicked   26
and turns back for them the wheel of fortune.

The LORD shines into a man's very soul,   27
searching out his inmost being.

A king's guards are loyalty and good faith,   28
his throne is upheld by righteousness.[b]

The glory of young men is their strength,   29
the dignity of old men their grey hairs.

A good beating purges the mind,   30
and blows chasten the inmost being.

✻ 2. *A king's threat*: the Hebrew has 'the terror inspired by a king'.

one who ignores it: this phrase has been rendered in various other ways, including 'he who draws it on himself'; 'he who irritates him'; 'he who loses his temper'. The general meaning of the saying is, however, fairly clear: like 16: 14, it reminds those who come into personal contact with the king that kings are not be treated like other men.

3. This saying is characteristic of the wisdom teacher's cautious attitude towards life: it is not the loud-mouthed fool who will make a lasting reputation, but the unobtrusive

[a] in his sight: *so Sept.; Heb. om.*
[b] *So Sept.; Heb.* loyalty.

person who steers clear of trouble. This kind of advice is frequent in non-Israelite Instructions, e.g. 'When you are confronted with a dispute, continue on your way; pay no attention to it' (*Counsels of Wisdom*, line 36).

4. *goes begging*: this word could also be translated 'looks expectantly': in spite of not having done the necessary work the lazy man expects results. This is a proverb about laziness in general, not confined in its application to a particular agricultural situation.

5. *in another's heart*: the Hebrew has 'in a man's heart', which would not exclude a reference to a man's own heart. The point seems to be that two things are necessary for the maturing of effective plans (*counsel*): the basic idea and its practical application. In other words, the educational ideal of the wisdom schools has no use for the dreamer or the pure intellectual, however brilliant: wisdom is essentially a practical accomplishment leading to success in life.

7. The view expressed here that divine blessing (as well as divine punishment) will be extended to one's descendants was a commonplace of Semitic belief. It receives classical expression in the second of the Ten Commandments (Exod. 20: 4–6).

8. See the note on 16: 10.

9. *I have a clear conscience*: literally, 'I have purified my heart'. It is presupposed that no one is free from sin, and the author goes on to assert that men are not even able to judge the sincerity of their own repentance: compare 16: 2.

10. See the note on 11: 1.

11. *innocent or guilty*: this translation follows the Septuagint. But the Hebrew 'innocent and upright' comes to the same thing.

young man: presumably the author would say that any man's character can be assessed by his actions. Perhaps the reason for singling out the *young* man was to suggest the additional idea that a man's character is formed early in life and does not change. See the note on 22: 6.

12. Since this saying makes a statement without drawing a

moral, more than one interpretation is possible. It could mean simply that the name of the maker guarantees the reliability of the product; but more probably it is intended to imply that since these organs were made so well they ought to be used properly. This is perhaps a teacher's exhortation to a pupil to pay attention.

14. *A bad bargain*: the Hebrew is more lively: 'No good! no good!' This is simply a humorous observation about business ethics in a country where haggling was an essential part of commerical life.

15. There is no intention here to despise wealth, but merely to observe that intelligent advice is so rare as to have a scarcity value exceeding that of precious metals and stones. Compare *Ptah-hotep*: 'Good speech is more hidden than the emerald.'

16. Although the precise situation envisaged here is not entirely clear, the transaction referred to comes under the heading of going surety, on which see the notes on 6: 1–5. The taking of a man's cloak as security for a straightforward loan was permitted under certain conditions (see Exod. 22: 26–7), and the saying asserts that this practice is equally justified in dealing with a man who goes surety for a third person.

17. This is a proverb of general application beyond its ostensible subject: wickedness does not pay in the long run.

18. This saying is similar to 11: 14, on which see the note, and 15: 22.

19. The first line is similar to that of 11: 13, on which see the note.

20. *reviles father and mother*: exactly the same phrase is used in the laws (e.g. Exod. 21: 17), where the punishment is death.

his lamp will go out: see the note on 13: 9. The phrase is a poetical expression for death, though probably with the additional implication that through the death of the individual the possibility of posterity is also removed. Compare *Ahikar*, line 138: 'As for the man who is not proud of the name of his father and mother, may the sun not shine upon him!'

21. On the first line see the N.E.B. footnote. There is some

doubt whether the reference is simply to 'getting rich quick', as in 13: 11, or whether some dishonest action, such as seizing an inheritance prematurely or illegitimately, is envisaged.

22. Compare 25: 21–2. Some non-Israelite texts similarly teach that one should not take vengeance, but the advice to *wait for the LORD to deliver you* is probably derived from Israelite teaching. Paul, in making the same point, quotes (in addition to Prov. 25: 21–2) a version of Deut. 32: 35: '"Justice is mine, says the Lord, I will repay"' (Rom. 12: 19–20). This principle is basic to all developed Jewish, and indeed to all civilized, thinking: the individual must not take private vengeance but leave God to carry out justice, perhaps through his appointed representatives.

23. Compare verse 10.

24. Compare 16: 1, 9; 19: 21; 27: 1. Each of these sayings has its own emphasis; here it is on man's ignorance of his destiny and his consequent dependence on God for guidance at each stage of his journey through life.

25. *dedicate a gift rashly*: the meaning of the phrase in the Hebrew is not entirely clear, but the second line indicates its general sense. There is a similar thought in Eccles. 5: 1–6. On the making of vows see the note on 7: 14. The wisdom principle that one should always avoid unconsidered action is here applied to the practice of religion.

26. The metaphor in the first line is the same as that employed in the second line of verse 8, and the general view of the king's infallible judgement is the same: see the note on 16: 10.

the wheel of fortune: the Hebrew has simply 'the wheel', and the translation of the N.E.B. is a guess: there are no other references to the wheel of fortune in the Old Testament. Another possible meaning is that the wheel is the wheel of the threshing-cart, which goes backwards and forwards over the grain to separate it from the chaff. This would fit well with the first line.

27. Literally translated the first line would read 'The breath of man is Yahweh's lamp'. This has been interpreted as

meaning that God in giving breath to man enables him to examine his own inner motives; but more probably it means that it is God who does this. The thought is then similar to that of 15: 11.

28. *loyalty and good faith*: these are terms which belong to the vocabulary of treaties and covenants. They are here personified as protectors of the king's person; in the second line *loyalty* (or *righteousness* according to the Septuagint) is said to be the support of the royal throne. The throne of the kings of Judah (see 1 Kings 10: 18–20) seems to have been partly modelled on the thrones of the kings of other Near Eastern countries, which in the details of their construction embodied various symbols of royal authority, especially its function as the means by which the divine Order was preserved in the world. There is a similar reference in Ps. 61: 6–7. In Judah this royal function was expressed in terms of the covenant or treaty concluded by God with David and his decendants (2 Sam. 7), and it may be that the words *loyalty and good faith* refer to this.

29. Compare 16: 31. Short of actual senility (for a picture of which see 1 Kings 1), the old were not regarded as 'past it' or 'out of touch'; on the contrary, they were highly respected because in a long life they were bound to have acquired more wisdom than the young.

30. This verse well expresses the rationale of corporal punishment: to give a *beating* is to apply externally a medicine which will have an internal and invisible effect on the character. See the note on 13: 24. ✳

The king's heart is under the LORD's hand;   **21**
like runnels of water, he turns it wherever he will.
A man may think that he is always right,   2
but the LORD fixes a standard for the heart.
Do what is right and just;   3
that is more pleasing to the LORD than sacrifice.

4   Haughty looks and a proud heart –
    these sins mark a wicked man.

5   Forethought and diligence are sure of profit;
    the man in a hurry is as sure of poverty.

6   He who makes a fortune by telling lies
    runs needlessly into the toils[a] of death.

7   The wicked are caught up in their own violence,
    because they refuse to do what is just.

8   The criminal's conduct is tortuous;
    straight dealing is a sign of integrity.

9   Better to live in a corner of the house-top
    than have a nagging wife and a brawling household.[b]

10 The wicked man is set on evil;
    he has no pity to spare for his friend.

11 The simple man is made wise when he sees the insolent
        punished,
    and learns his lesson when the wise man prospers.

12 The just God[c] makes the wicked man's home childless;[d]
    he overturns the wicked and ruins them.

13 If a man shuts his ears to the cry of the helpless,
    he will cry for help himself and not be heard.

14 A gift in secret placates an angry man;
    a bribe slipped under the cloak pacifies great wrath.

15 When justice is done, all good men rejoice,
    but it brings ruin to evildoers.

16 A man who takes leave of common sense
    comes to rest in the company of the dead.

17 Love pleasure and you will beg your bread;
    a man who loves wine and oil will never grow rich.

[a] into the toils: *prob. rdg.*, *cp. Sept.*; *Heb.* the seekers.
[b] and a brawling household: *or, with slight change of consonants*, in a spacious house.
[c] *Or* The just man.
[d] makes...childless: *prob. rdg.*; *Heb.* considers the wicked man's home.

The wicked man serves as a ransom for the righteous, 18
so does a traitor for the upright.

Better to live alone in the desert 19
than with a nagging and ill-tempered wife.

The wise man has his home full of fine and costly 20
  treasures;
the stupid man is a mere spendthrift.

Persevere in right conduct and loyalty 21
and you shall find life*a* and honour.

A wise man climbs into a city full of armed men 22
and undermines its strength and its confidence.

Keep a guard over your lips and tongue 23
and keep yourself out of trouble.

The conceited man is haughty, his name is insolence; 24
conceit and impatience are in all he does.

The sluggard's cravings will be the death of him, 25
because his hands refuse to work;
all day long his cravings go unsatisfied, 26
while the righteous man gives without stint.

The wicked man's sacrifice is an abomination to the 27
  LORD;*b*
how much more when he offers it with vileness at
  heart!

A lying witness will perish, 28
but he whose words ring true will leave children behind
  him.

A wicked man puts a bold face on it, 29
whereas the upright man secures his line of retreat.*c*

Face to face with the LORD, 30
wisdom, understanding, counsel go for nothing.

[a] *So Sept.; Heb. adds* righteousness.
[b] to the LORD: *so Sept.; Heb. om.*
[c] secures...retreat: *or, as otherwise read,* considers his conduct.

31   A horse may be made ready for the day of battle,
     but victory comes from the LORD.

* 1–2. Two more sayings stressing God's control of human life.

1. The recognition that the king, like other men, is subject
to God's control does not contradict those sayings (e.g. 16: 10)
which seem to suggest that he has superhuman powers. The
king was seen as God's agent or representative.

The king's heart: as in other passages, *heart* means the intelligence and the will.

runnels of water: the metaphor is taken from the process of
irrigation by means of artificial dams and canals.

2. See the note on 16: 2.

3. On this sentiment see the note on 15: 8. The point is not
that sacrifice is wrong or unnecessary, but that other things
are more important to God.

4. The N.E.B. translation of the second line of this saying
is conjectural. In Hebrew it appears to mean 'the ploughland
of the wicked is sin'. A slight alteration would yield the meaning 'lamp' instead of 'ploughland', and this is how the
Septuagint understood it.

6. *toils of death*: this translation is based on a widely accepted
alteration of the Hebrew text, which has the meaningless
'seekers after death'. The phrase 'snares (or toils) of death'
occurs in Ps. 18: 5. Death is seen here in personal terms as one
who snares men as a hunter snares animals. This metaphor
probably has mythological origins.

7. *caught up*: that is, in a snare. The metaphor is the same as
that used in verse 6.

9. *a brawling household*: other possible translations are 'a
shared house', 'a spacious house' and 'an alehouse'.

10. *his friend*: the word in Hebrew means 'neighbour', that
is, any person with whom a man comes into frequent contact.
The question whether wicked men have friends, and if so
what sort of people they are, is not raised here.

12. In the first line of this saying the N.E.B. translators

have tried to make sense of a difficult line (on the Hebrew see the footnotes) by taking the adjective *just* as referring to God (as it does in Job 34: 17) and slightly emending the verb.

14. On this attitude towards bribery, which agrees with 17: 8; 18: 16 against 15: 27; 17: 23, see the note on 17:8. We should note that the author expresses no opinion on the propriety of the practice, although this is probably implied.

16. This saying is open to more than one interpretation. It may mean that folly leads to a premature death, or that the fool is already as good as dead, since his lack of wisdom deprives him of those advantages and pleasures which constitute 'life' in the fullest sense.

17. *wine and oil*: these are symbols of indulgence in lavish entertainment.

18. This saying has been interpreted in two opposite ways. The word *ransom* implies that the wicked man is in some sense substituted for the righteous, but there is nothing to indicate whether the circumstances which the author has in mind are good or bad. If the saying means that *the wicked man* often gets the good things of life which ought to go to the *upright* man it is a despairing plea for justice for those who are wronged. This point of view is found elsewhere, especially in Job, but it is at variance with the usual teaching of Proverbs, and it is more likely that the meaning is similar to that of 11: 8: the wicked man is *a ransom for the righteous* in the sense that he suffers the evil fate which he has prepared for him.

19. Compare verse 9.

20. Compare verse 17.

fine and costly treasures: the usual translation of the Hebrew is 'fine treasures and oil'; but the meaning is not affected.

21. The word which the N.E.B. translators have omitted (see the footnote) is the same as that translated by *right conduct* in the first line. Its repetition is clearly a scribal error.

22. Compare 16: 32, on which see the note. The saying is not, of course, to be taken literally, but means that the real captor of a city is not the soldier who actually climbs the wall

but the general who plans the operation. Real power lies in the hands of the man with the brains, who does not need to exert himself physically. Compare *Merikare*: 'Speech is more powerful than any fighting.'

23. See the note on 13: 3, and compare *Counsels of Wisdom*, lines 26–7:

> Let your mouth be controlled and your speech guarded:
> therein lies a man's wealth – let your lips be very precious.

24. The reason for giving a list of almost synonymous unpleasant characteristics here is not clear. Possibly the intention was to define the term *insolence*, which occurs frequently in this section and may have been a technical term.

25–6. The N.E.B. translators take these two verses as constituting a single saying, but they could be translated as two separate sayings. Verse 25 makes the same point as 19: 24. Verse 26 is not wholly intelligible, but the second line makes the point that one of the characteristics of *the righteous man* is generosity to those in need.

27. See the note on 15: 8 and compare 21: 3.

with vileness at heart: it is not quite clear what additional wickedness is meant here. Possibly a man might offer sacrifice with some specific evil intention in mind, such as the giving of a false impression to others of his piety.

28. The natural translation of the second line of this saying would be 'but the man who listens will speak for ever'. This does not make sense. The translation of the N.E.B., which is based on somewhat speculative interpretations of some of the words, is one of a number of attempts to produce a line which will make sense in relation to the first line.

29. Here again the relationship between the two lines is difficult to understand. The Hebrew text of the second line offers two alternatives: 'understands his way(s)' or 'establishes his way(s)'. The N.E.B. translators have accepted the second alternative, interpreting 'way' as meaning *line of retreat*. This is to read a good deal into the word, and does not suggest con-

duct particularly characteristic of a righteous man. An alternative solution would be to accept the meaning 'establishes his way', taking 'way' in the sense of 'way of life, conduct'. The difference between the *wicked* and the *upright man* would then be that whereas the former relies on bluff and deceit, the latter relies on his own good actions to establish his reputation.

30–1. Two more sayings emphasizing God's sovereignty.

30. Compare 16: 1, 3, 9; 19: 21; 20: 24. This saying belongs to the category of those which recognize that even the greatest achievements of the wisdom schools are valueless unless they are seen to be subject to the approval of God. ✻

A good name is more to be desired than great riches; **22**
esteem is better than silver or gold.

Rich and poor have this in common: 2
the LORD made them both.

A shrewd man sees trouble coming and lies low; 3
the simple walk into it and pay the penalty.

The fruit of humility is the fear of God 4
with riches and honour and life.

The crooked man's path is set with snares and pitfalls; 5
the cautious man will steer clear of them.

Start a boy on the right road, 6
and even in old age he will not leave it.

The rich lord it over the poor; 7
the borrower becomes the lender's slave.

The man who sows injustice reaps trouble, 8
and the end of his work[a] will be the rod.[b]

The kindly man will be blessed, 9
for he shares his food with the poor.

Drive out the insolent man, and strife goes with him; 10
if he sits on the bench, he makes a mockery of justice.[c]

[a] So Sept.; Heb. his wrath.   [b] the rod: or the threshing.
[c] if...justice: prob. rdg., cp. Sept.; Heb. and disgraceful litigation will cease.

11 The LORD*ᵃ* loves a sincere man;
but you will make a king your friend with your fine
phrases.

12 The LORD keeps watch over every claim at law,
and overturns the scoundrel's case.

13 The sluggard protests, 'There's a lion outside;
I shall get myself killed in the street.'

14 The words of an adulteress are like a deep pit;
those whom the LORD has cursed will fall into it.

15 Folly is deep-rooted in the heart of a boy;
a good beating will drive it right out of him.

16 Oppression of the poor may bring gain to a man,
but giving to the rich leads only to penury.

✵ 1. *A good name*: see the note on 10: 7.

2. It is characteristic of Israelite wisdom literature to base
an argument on the fact of creation; but as in 20: 12 the
writer is content to state the facts and to leave the reader to
draw his own moral.

6. The wisdom teachers, like the Jesuits in a later age, were
supremely confident of the character-forming quality of their
system of education.

7. This is another example of the type of saying which simply points to the facts of life and leaves the reader to draw a
moral if he wishes.

8. The second line of this saying is difficult: presumably it
originally offered a thought parallel to that of the first line,
but the Hebrew text 'and the rod of his fury will fail' hardly
meets the case. The N.E.B. translators have chosen one solution among many in assuming a slight textual error, correcting
'fury' to *work*, a translation which is in line with the Septuagint. In their footnote they have offered 'the threshing' as an
alternative to *the rod*: this would preserve the agricultural
metaphor of the first line.

[a] The LORD: *so Sept.; Heb. om.*

9. Generosity to the poor was recognized as a virtue both in Israel and throughout the ancient Near East. Compare Job 31: 16–22 and also *Papyrus Insinger* xv 16: 13: 'He who gives food to the poor will receive the infinite mercy of God.'

10. In the second line of this saying the N.E.B. translators considered that the Hebrew – of which they give a translation in the footnote – is unsatisfactory, and have slightly altered the text. Whether the Hebrew is unsatisfactory is a matter of opinion: *the insolent man*, who delights in *strife*, would be likely to engage in 'disgraceful litigation', in which he gratuitously drags the innocent man through the courts.

11. The Hebrew of this saying is almost impossible to translate. The N.E.B. translators have followed the Septuagint in the first line by adding *The LORD*; in the second line the meaning is probably something like the N.E.B. rendering, but the grammar is difficult.

12. *every claim at law*: this is an unusual translation of a word which is normally translated by 'knowledge'. The statement that God's eyes 'keep watch over knowledge' would be similar to 15: 3.

13. Compare 19: 24. The lazy man who makes absurd excuses for not going out to work is a figure of fun as well as a warning to others. This is an admirable example of the wisdom writer's ability to suggest an entire scene in a few words.

14. The theme is the same as that of the warnings against the *adulteress* in chapters 2, 5, 6 and 7. In 23: 27 the woman herself is described as a 'deep pit'.

15. This saying complements verse 6 in setting out the educational theory of the wisdom teachers. Education is not merely a question of bringing out the pupil's potentialities, but involves the suppression of the *folly* which is inherent in him. This might be described as a doctrine of 'original folly'.

16. In the N.E.B. translation this saying, the Hebrew of which is so compressed as to be enigmatic, seems merely to be a rather feeble statement of the obvious. Another interpretation is possible: the *gain* may be that of the *poor* who is

oppressed rather than that of the oppressor, and the *penury* the fate of the *rich* who receives the gift rather than that of the giver. If this interpretation is correct, the saying asserts that men's evil intentions and actions are reversed by a beneficent Order: the oppression inflicted on the poor will mysteriously be turned into his triumph, and the gifts exacted by the rich will somehow be the cause of his downfall. The first of these propositions is illustrated by the career of Joseph (Gen. 37–50), who in the time of his success is able to express the same thought in the words 'You meant to do me harm; but God meant to bring good out of it' (Gen. 50: 20).

SECTION III. PROVERBS 22: 17–24: 22

Thirty wise sayings

THE SAYINGS OF THE WISE

17 THE SAYINGS of the wise:

Pay heed and listen to my words,[a]
open your mind to the knowledge I impart;
18 to keep them in your heart will be a pleasure,
and then you will always have them ready on your lips.
19 I would have you trust in the LORD
and so I tell you these things this day for your own good.
20 Here I have written out for you thirty sayings,
full of knowledge and wise advice,
21 to impart to you a knowledge of the truth,
that you may take back a true report[b] to him who sent you.

[a] my words: *prob. rdg.*, *cp. Sept.*; *Heb. om.*
[b] *Prob. rdg.*; *Heb. adds* words of truth.

Never rob a helpless man because he is helpless,[a]   22
nor ill-treat a poor wretch in court;
for the LORD will take up their cause   23
and rob him who robs them of their livelihood.
Never make friends with an angry man   24
nor keep company with a bad-tempered one;
be careful not to learn his ways,   25
or you will find yourself caught in a trap.
Never be one to give guarantees,   26
or to pledge yourself as surety for another;
for if you cannot pay, beware: 27
your bed will be taken from under you.
Do not move the ancient boundary-stone   28
which your forefathers set up.
You see a man skilful at his craft: 29
he will serve kings, he will not serve common men.

When you sit down to eat with a ruling prince,   **23**
be sure to keep your mind on what is before you,
and if you are a greedy man,   2
cut your throat first.
Do not be greedy for his dainties,   3
for they are not what they seem.
Do not slave to get wealth;[b]   4
be a sensible man, and give up.
Before you can look round, it will be gone;   5
it will surely grow wings
like an eagle, like a bird in the sky.
Do not go to dinner with a miser,[c]   6
do not be greedy for his dainties;

[a] helpless: *lit*. a door (*cp. Song of Songs 8: 9*); *there is a play on words in the Heb.*
[b] to get wealth: *or* for an invitation to a feast.
[c] *Or* a man with an evil eye.

7   for they will stick in your^a throat like a hair.
    He will bid you eat and drink,
    but his heart is not with you;
8   you will bring up the mouthful you have eaten,
    and your winning words will have been wasted.

9   Hold your tongue in the hearing of a stupid man;
    for he will despise your words of wisdom.
10 Do not move the ancient boundary-stone
    or encroach on the land of orphans:
11 they have a powerful guardian
    who will take up their cause against you.
12 Apply your mind to instruction
    and open your ears to knowledge when it speaks.
13 Do not withhold discipline from a boy;
    take the stick to him, and save him from death.
14 If you take the stick to him yourself,
    you will preserve him from the jaws of death.^b
15 My son, if you are wise at heart,
    my heart in its turn will be glad;
16 I shall rejoice with all my soul
    when you speak plain truth.

17 Do not try to emulate sinners;
    envy only those who fear the LORD day by day;
18 do this,^c and you may look forward to the future,^d
    and your thread of life will not be cut short.

19 Listen, my son, listen, and become wise;
    set your mind on the right course.
20 Do not keep company with drunkards

[a] *Prob. rdg.; Heb.* his.
[b] the jaws of death: *Heb.* Sheol.
[c] do this: *prob. rdg., cp. Sept.; Heb. om.*
[d] and...future: *so Sept.; Heb.* and there will be a future.

128

or those who are greedy for the fleshpots;
for drink and greed will end in poverty,   21
and drunken stupor goes in rags.

Listen to your father, who gave you life,   22
and do not despise your mother when she is old.
Buy truth, never sell it;   23
buy wisdom, instruction, and understanding.
A good man's father will rejoice   24
and he who has a wise son will delight in him.
Give your father and your mother cause for delight,   25
let her who bore you rejoice.

My son, mark my words,   26
and accept my guidance with a will.
A prostitute is a deep pit,   27
a loose woman a narrow well;
she lies in wait like a robber   28
and betrays her husband with man after man.

Whose is the misery? whose the remorse?   29
Whose are the quarrels and the anxiety?
Who gets the bruises without knowing why?
Whose eyes are bloodshot?
Those who linger late over their wine,   30
those who are always trying some new spiced liquor.
Do not gulp down the wine, the strong red wine,   31
when the droplets form on the side of the cup;[a]
in the end it will bite like a snake   32
and sting like a cobra.
Then your eyes see strange sights,   33
your wits and your speech are confused;
you become like a man tossing out at sea,   34

[a] *Prob. rdg.; Heb. adds* it runs smoothly to and fro.

like one who clings to[a] the top of the rigging;
35   you say, 'If it lays me flat, what do I care?
If it brings me to the ground, what of it?
As soon as I wake up,
I shall turn to it again.'[b]

24   Do not emulate wicked men
or long to make friends with them;
2   for violence is all they think of,
and all they say means mischief.

3   Wisdom builds the house,
good judgement makes it secure,
4   knowledge furnishes the rooms
with all the precious and pleasant things that wealth
    can buy.

5   Wisdom prevails over strength,
knowledge over brute force;
6   for wars are won by skilful strategy,
and victory is the fruit of long planning.

7   Wisdom is too high for a fool;
he dare not open his mouth in court.

8   A man who is bent on mischief
gets a name for intrigue;
9   the intrigues of foolish men misfire,
and the insolent man is odious to his fellows.

10   If your strength fails on a lucky[c] day,
how helpless will you be on a day[d] of disaster!

[a] clings to: *prob. rdg.; Heb.* lies on.
[b] turn to it again: *or, with Sept.,* seek my boon companions.
[c] lucky: *prob. rdg.; Heb. om.*
[d] a day: *prob. rdg., cp. Sept.; Heb. om.*

When you see a man being dragged to be killed, go to 11
   his rescue,
and save those being hurried away to their death.
If you say, 'But I*ᵃ* do not know this man',   12
God, who fixes a standard for the heart, will take note.
God who watches you – be sure he will know;
he will requite every man for what he does.

Eat honey, my son, for it is good,   13
and the honeycomb so sweet upon the tongue.
Make wisdom too your own;   14
if you find it, you may look forward to the future,
and your thread of life will not be cut short.

Do not lie in wait like a felon at the good man's house, 15
or raid his farm.
Though the good man may fall seven times, he is soon 16
   up again,
but the rascal is brought down by misfortune.
Do not rejoice when your enemy falls,   17
do not gloat when he is brought down;
or the LORD will see and be displeased with you,   18
and he will cease to be angry with him.

Do not vie with evildoers   19
or emulate the wicked;
for wicked men have no future to look forward to;   20
their embers will be put out.

My son, fear the LORD and grow rich,   21
but have nothing to do with men of rank,
they will bring about disaster without warning;   22
who knows what ruin such men may cause?*ᵇ*

[a] *So Sept.; Heb.* we.
[b] they...cause: *or* they will come to sudden disaster; who knows what
the ruin of such men will be.

✴ The heading in the N.E.B. applies only to 22: 17–24: 22. The thirty sayings are preceded by an introduction (22: 17–21). There are some differences of opinion about their exact demarcation in some cases.

It can hardly be a coincidence that *Amen-em-opet* also has thirty chapters preceded by an introduction. The two works have more in common than their form. In the first part of the biblical work (up to 23: 11) almost every theme corresponds wholly or in part to a chapter in *Amen-em-opet*, although the order is different. There are numerous verbal similarities between the two works, and there can be no doubt that one is directly dependent on the other. Although the dates of neither can be fixed exactly, it is almost certain that it was the Israelite author who knew and made use of the Egyptian work. But the former is neither a direct translation nor a slavish imitation of its Egyptian model.

The fact that it is only in the first part that direct parallels with *Amen-em-opet* are found is difficult to explain. It can hardly be that the Israelite author knew of only part of the Egyptian work, since the material which he has used comes from almost every part of it. It may be that he began by making what use he could of it, and then, unable to find enough material in it suitable for his purpose, turned to other sources. In particular he seems to have made use of *Ahikar*. Other sayings have a distinctly Israelite flavour, some are of a vague and general nature, and there is some repetition. The work thus lacks the consistency of its Egyptian model.

22: 17–21. The introduction. *Amen-em-opet* contains three sections which are comparable with this: a general preface (1: 1–12), an introduction (chapter 1) and an epilogue (chapter xxx). All three contain striking parallels with these verses.

17. *The sayings of the wise*: in the Hebrew this heading is misplaced and embedded in the next sentence, but there can be little doubt that the N.E.B. translators have restored it to its proper place as the heading of the whole section. It is not,

however, original, but an editorial addition made when the various sections of the book were joined together. This can be seen from the fact that in the introduction (verses 17–20) it is a single author (not *the wise* in general) who is speaking.

Pay heed: literally, 'incline your ear'; *your mind*: literally, 'your heart'. These two lines are very similar to *Amen-em-opet* I 3: 9–10.

> Give your ears, listen to what is said,
> give your heart to understand it.

18. Compare *Amen-em-opet* I 3: 11: 'To put them in your heart is good.'

19. This verse is a distinctively Israelite contribution.

20. Compare the epilogue of *Amen-em-opet* (XXX 27: 7–10):

> See for yourself these thirty chapters:
> they entertain; they educate;
> they are the foremost of all books;
> they instruct the ignorant.

21. Compare the purpose of the thirty chapters according to the preface to *Amen-em-opet* (1: 5–7):

> To know how to return an answer to him who has spoken,
> and to return a report to one who has sent him,
> to direct him to the paths of life.

In both cases the situation envisaged is that of the court official entrusted by his superior with the conveying of messages and the answers to them. In view of the contents of the teaching which follows both in Proverbs and in *Amen-em-opet* this may seem a rather strange way of commending the usefulness of the book, but the ability to discharge this important function in a reliable manner was a test of character, and it was just such a reliable character which it was the purpose of such Instructions as these to form. That this particular detail should appear in both works is a striking illustration of the direct dependence of the one on the other.

22–3. THE FIRST SAYING corresponds to chapter II of *Amen-em-opet*, which begins

> Beware of robbing the helpless
> and of ill-treating the disabled.   (II 4: 4–5)

Like the Israelite author, *Amen-em-opet* teaches that such a crime will receive divine punishment: the poor man's 'voice reaches to heaven' (II 4: 18).

24–5. THE SECOND SAYING corresponds to chapter IX of *Amen-em-opet*, which begins

> Do not associate with a hothead
> nor visit him for conversation   (IX 11: 13–14)

and ends

> lest a terror carry you off.   (IX 13: 9)

On the theme see the note on 17: 27.

26–7. THE THIRD SAYING has no parallel in *Amen-em-opet*. On the situation envisaged see the notes on 6: 1–5.

28. THE FOURTH SAYING corresponds to chapter VI of *Amen-em-opet*, though the subject is a frequent one also in the Old Testament. See the note on 15: 25.

29. THE FIFTH SAYING finds its parallel in the epilogue of *Amen-em-opet*:

> As for the scribe who is experienced in his craft,
> he will find himself worthy to be a courtier.
>
> (XXX 27: 16–17)

The *craft* referred to here is clearly that of the accomplished scribe or official.

23: 1–3. THE SIXTH SAYING. *Amen-em-opet* (chapter XXIII) goes even further:

> Do not eat bread in the presence of a nobleman.
>
> (XXIII 23: 13)

The theme occurs in other Egyptian Instructions, e.g. *Ptah-hotep*: 'If you are among the guests of a man of higher rank, take what he offers when it is presented to you.'

2. *cut your throat first*: literally, 'put a knife to your throat'. This probably means 'curb your appetite'.

3. *they are not what they seem*: this may mean that there is some sinister motive behind the invitation, or perhaps merely that one's table manners are bound to be observed by others and taken into account when promotion is being considered.

4–5. THE SEVENTH SAYING is very close to chapter VII of *Amen-em-opet*, which begins

Do not set your heart on the pursuit of riches,
for it is impossible to ignore Fate and Fortune

(VII 9: 10–11)

and contains the lines

They have made themselves wings like geese
and have flown away to heaven. (VII 10: 4–5)

There is no disparagement of wealth here, but a warning not to *slave* (literally, 'wear yourself out') in an attempt to acquire something which is notoriously ephemeral.

6–8. THE EIGHTH SAYING, which has some affinities with the sixth, has no real parallel with *Amen-em-opet*, although some of the imagery is close to that used by *Amen-em-opet* on a different subject.

6. *a miser*: literally, 'a man with an evil eye'. The same phrase is used in 28: 22.

7. *they will stick in your throat like a hair*: this, which is based on a slight alteration of the text, is perhaps the most likely translation of a difficult line. *Amen-em-opet*, in a chapter warning against coveting the property of the poor, uses a similar expression: such property, if it is attained, will be 'a blocking of the throat' (XI 14: 7). See also the note on verse 8.

8. Compare *Amen-em-opet*, in the lines which immediately follow the quotation just given:

It makes the gullet vomit...
The mouthful of bread which is too big you swallow
    but vomit up,
and so lose a good thing.   (XI 14: 8, 17–18)

9. THE NINTH SAYING: there is no real parallel in *Amen-em-opet*, although the Egyptian work does have a warning, common enough in the wisdom literature, against being too free with one's speech. But compare *Onchsheshonqy* 7: 3–4:

Do not instruct a fool, lest he hate you.
Do not give instruction to a man who will not listen to you.

10–11. THE TENTH SAYING: the first line is identical with the first line of the fourth saying, on which see the note.

11. In Israelite law the *guardian* was the kinsman whose duty it was to intervene in the case of financial crisis to prevent family property from being sold outside the family (see the law in Lev. 25: 25, where the word is translated 'next-of-kin'). Here it is God who is the guardian of those who have no such human protector. *take up their cause* is a phrase taken from legal practice.

12. This verse is regarded by some commentators as constituting the eleventh saying, but it is more probably a later addition, perhaps taken from some other context; or it may be simply a variant of 22: 17, on which see the note.

13–14. THE ELEVENTH SAYING is strikingly similar to *Ahikar*, lines 81–2: 'Do not spare your son the rod, or you will be unable to save him from wickedness. *If I strike you, my son, you will not die*, but if I leave you to your own devices you will not live.' The words in italics are almost identical with the second line of verse 13, of which a literal translation would be 'When you strike him with the rod he will not die.' It is not certain whether this 'death' refers to the physical effects of the beating, or, as in the second line of verse 14, to the retribution which will fall upon an undisciplined person (as the N.E.B. translators take it to mean).

15–16. THE TWELFTH SAYING: this is the first of a number of rather general sayings which stand side by side with more concrete pieces of advice.

17–18. THE THIRTEENTH SAYING.

18. *do this*: these words are not represented in the Hebrew, but a verb is necessary to complete the line. That such a verb stood in the original text is made probable by a comparison with 24: 14.

thread of life: a more usual translation of this word is 'hope'.

19–21. THE FOURTEENTH SAYING: on drunkenness and gluttony. These, like every form of excess, are frequently condemned by the wisdom writers.

22–5. These verses deal with general matters. Although certainty is not possible on matters of this kind, verse 23, which ought perhaps to be taken with verse 19, seems to be an intrusion.

22, 24–5. THE FIFTEENTH SAYING: this is in line with the Fifth Commandment (Exod. 20: 12); but reverence for parents was regarded as a duty of prime importance throughout the ancient Near East. Similarly parents' pride in their sons was even greater than it is today, since it was believed that a man's life had some kind of continuation in the lives of his children.

23. THE SIXTEENTH SAYING: compare 4: 7. This saying is probably independent of foreign influence.

26–8. THE SEVENTEENTH SAYING: avoidance of sexual immorality.

26. Such introductory sentences with which some of the thirty sayings begin are reminiscent of the introductions to the Instructions in chapters 1–9, and suggest that some of these sayings may originally have been independent pieces.

my guidance: literally, 'my ways'. This could equally well be interpreted as meaning 'my conduct', in which case the teacher would be recommending the pupil to imitate himself.

27. Compare 22: 14.

28. *lies in wait*: compare the description of the woman lurking at the corner of the street in 7: 12.

and betrays her husband with man after man: the meaning of the
Hebrew is not certain.

29–35. THE EIGHTEENTH SAYING: a vivid portrait of the
drunkard, based on acute observation and psychological
insight. In length it is comparable with the description of the
adulteress in 7: 6–23. Such passages show that some wisdom
teachers were sufficiently skilled to break away from the
traditional form of the short saying and make effective use of
their imagination. Such longer passages are characteristic of
the Egyptian Instruction.

29. It has been suggested that the series of questions, to
which the answer is given in verse 30, is based on the custom
of riddling (see the note on 1: 6). But whether this is so or not
it is used here for another purpose: to emphasize the effects
of drunkenness in the most telling way possible.

31. *Do not gulp down*: this makes better sense than the more
usual translation 'do not look at the wine', which is probably
based on a confusion of two similar verbs.

droplets: the Hebrew has 'when it makes an "eye" in the
cup'. The problem is of the exact metaphorical sense which
'eye' has here. 'When it sparkles in the cup' is another possible translation.

The additional line in the Hebrew, referred to in the N.E.B.
footnote, may be an allusion added by a reader to Song of
Songs 7: 9, where wine is described as 'flowing smoothly'.

33–5. These verses describe the sensations of a drunken
man: hallucination, inability to speak properly, the feeling that
the gound is heaving and the loss of a sense of responsibility.

34. *tossing out at sea*: literally, 'lying down in the heart of
the sea'. The N.E.B. has slightly changed the text here, but the
Hebrew makes good sense. The drunkard, who has lain down
on the floor because he is unable to stand up, feels that the
ground under him is heaving like the sea.

clings to the top of the rigging: the Hebrew has 'lies down on
the top of the rigging'. Here the textual change made by the
N.E.B. translators seems more justified.

35. In the first half of the verse the Hebrew has 'They struck me but I was not hurt; they beat me but I did not notice it'. This seems perfectly satisfactory.

24: 1–2. THE NINETEENTH SAYING: the theme is reminiscent of 1: 10–19, and the first line of verse 1 is similar to 23: 17.

3–4. THE TWENTIETH SAYING: in the Hebrew the verbs are passive: 'Through wisdom a house is built' etc. The question is whether wisdom is personified or not. The saying may mean merely that it is by acquiring wisdom that a man succeeds in life, gaining the means to build a substantial home and to furnish it lavishly. On the other hand we ought to bear in mind that in 9: 1 Wisdom is personified as a woman who builds a house and invites men to come and share a feast which will make them wise and so confer on them the gift of 'life'. But whether there is personification here or not, the saying asserts that wisdom is the key to success.

5–6. THE TWENTY-FIRST SAYING: the second half (verse 6) is a variant of 11: 14; 20: 18. This saying as a whole therefore looks like an expansion of a shorter saying or the result of the combination of two shorter sayings. This fact is interesting as showing how longer wisdom pieces may have been built up.

5. The Hebrew makes no sense here: the N.E.B. translators have attempted a reconstruction along the lines of the ancient Versions.

7. THE TWENTY-SECOND SAYING.

in court: literally, 'in the gate'. The N.E.B. translation unduly limits the meaning. See the note on 1: 21. The point is that the fool who has not learned wisdom will not be accorded any standing in the community.

8–9. THE TWENTY-THIRD SAYING.

9. *misfire*: the usual translation of this word would be 'are sinful'.

10. THE TWENTY-FOURTH SAYING: the point of this saying seems to be the importance of perseverance. The N.E.B. translators have added the word *lucky* and changed the order of the words in order to provide a contrast between the two

lines. The Hebrew reads 'If you show weakness on a day of disaster, your strength is small'. If the Hebrew is correct, there is a play on words here, the Hebrew words for 'disaster' and 'small' being similar.

11–12. THE TWENTY-FIFTH SAYING: this can hardly refer to convicted prisoners being taken to the place of execution: such advice would be both immoral and unrealistic. It refers to violence in the street. Then as now bystanders often made no move to help the victims as they did not want to become involved. This saying condemns this lack of social solidarity and regards it as a sin which God will punish.

12. *fixes a standard for the heart*: see the note on 16:2.

will requite every man for what he does: a perfect expression of basic wisdom doctrine.

13–14. THE TWENTY-SIXTH SAYING: the intention of this saying seems to be to compare the pleasure conferred by wisdom with the taste of honey, which was a symbol of anything pleasant: compare 5: 3; 16: 24. Unfortunately the first line of verse 14 has been imperfectly preserved, and what was no doubt originally an effective comparison has been spoiled. The N.E.B. translators have done their best with it, but the line is metrically too short, and some words have probably fallen out. The last two lines are almost identical with 23: 18.

15–16. THE TWENTY-SEVENTH SAYING: violence does not pay.

16. *seven times*: this means an indefinite number of times. The point is that *the good man* may suffer temporary misfortune at the hands of *the rascal*, but virtue will triumph in the end.

17–18. THE TWENTY-EIGHTH SAYING.

17. The *enemy* is a personal, not a national, one. This is no contest between the good man and the wicked, in which God is inevitably wholly on the one side, but a petty feud of which he is the arbiter, but inclined to side with the underdog.

19–20. THE TWENTY-NINTH SAYING: this is a variant of 23: 17–18. Compare the second line of verse 20 with that of 13: 9, on which see the note.

21–2. THE THIRTIETH SAYING: the N.E.B. translators have completely altered the meaning of this saying. In the first line of verse 21 the Hebrew has 'Fear Yahweh and the king'. This last word has been altered to give the verb 'grow rich'. It is questionable whether this alteration makes the line any less difficult. The Hebrew text reflects on the fact that Israelite kings, like the kings of other ancient Near Eastern peoples, were regarded as the representatives of God and endowed with his authority. The word translated *men of rank* is of doubtful meaning, and this makes it difficult either to understand what kind of contrast is intended between the lines of this verse, or the reason given for avoiding them in verse 22. ✴

SECTION IV. PROVERBS 24: 23–34

MORE SAYINGS OF WISE MEN

More sayings of wise men: 23

Partiality in dispensing justice is not good.
A judge who pronounces a guilty man innocent   24
is cursed by all nations, all peoples execrate him;
but for those who convict the guilty all will go well, 25
they will be blessed with prosperity.
A straightforward answer   26
is as good as a kiss of friendship.

First put all in order out of doors   27
and make everything ready on the land;
then establish your house and home.

Do not be a witness against your neighbour without 28
    good reason
nor misrepresent him in your evidence.
Do not say,   29

'I will do to him what he has done to me;
I will requite him for what he has done.'

30   I passed by the field of an idle man,
     by the vineyard of a man with no sense.

31   I looked, and it was all dried up,[a]
     it was overgrown with thistles
     and covered with weeds,
     and the stones of its walls had been torn down.

32   I saw and I took good note,
     I considered and learnt the lesson:

33   a little sleep, a little slumber,
       a little folding of the hands in rest,

34   and poverty will come upon you like a robber,
       want like a ruffian.

---

* The heading at the beginning of verse 23 (literally, 'These also are words of wise men') indicates that at some stage this section was attached to 22: 17–24: 22 as a kind of appendix. It was originally an independent section, and in the Septuagint, where several of the sections in the book are placed in a different order from that of the Hebrew, the two sections are not consecutive but are separated by chapters 25–31. This section belongs to the same general type as 22: 17–24: 22 in that it contains longer pieces as well as two-line sayings.

23–9. These sayings are mainly, though not entirely, concerned with the ethical principles governing behaviour in the lawcourts. These principles do not differ from those generally acknowledged in the ancient Near East, as is clear from their frequent occurrence in both the laws and the wisdom literature of Israel and of its neighbours.

23. Compare 18: 5. This saying is addressed to judges or future judges.

24–5. This saying also is addressed to judges. It is taken for

[a] and...dried up: *prob. rdg.*, *cp. Sept.*; *Heb. om.*

granted that all civilized nations have certain ethical principles in common.

26. This saying is also relevant to behaviour in the lawcourt, but its meaning is not restricted to this. Whether in the witness box or in ordinary human relationships, true friendship is characterized by truthfulness.

27. This saying seems to be unrelated to those around it. It is a true proverb in that its application extends beyond its literal meaning. On the literal level it is a warning to the young farmer to get his priorities right: he must make sure that his land is in good order and producing enough to live on before he can think of settling down in comfort. *establish your house and home* is simply 'build your house' in Hebrew, a phrase which includes the ideas both of putting up a house and starting a family. There is no reason to suppose that this saying is specifically addressed to people working on the land: its meaning is 'first things first'.

28. This saying is concerned with the giving of evidence in court, but its meaning is not entirely clear. *without good reason* may refer to the man who maliciously denounces other people to the authorities, or to the man who, when called to give evidence, tells lies out of spite. The meaning of the word translated *misrepresent* is uncertain.

29. It is not clear whether this saying is the continuation of verse 28 or not. In any case it strongly condemns the taking of revenge, and so may be compared with the teaching of Jesus in Matt. 5: 43-5. But we cannot give credit to the Israelites for the establishment of this ethical principle: see the note on 25: 21-2.

30-4. This little story belongs to a quite different type of wisdom literature from the preceding verses: that of the wisdom teacher's personal reminiscence. Other examples in Proverbs are 4: 1-5; 7: 6-23, on which see the notes; compare also Ps. 37: 35-6. These reminiscences are fictitious: the narrative form is simply a teaching device. In this passage the theme is the same as that of 6: 6-11, and these passages both conclude with virtually the same words (6: 10–11; 24: 33–4), although in other respects the treatment is quite different. This gives us an insight into the way in which the wisdom teachers elaborated traditional material: two teachers independently created lively material out of the same older saying. *

SECTION V. PROVERBS 25–9

(In the N.E.B. this whole section and sections VI and VII form a single section.)

Other collections of wise sayings

FURTHER PROVERBS OF SOLOMON

Chapters 25–9 are grouped together as one section by the editor who provided the headings to this (25: 1) and the following (30: 1) sections; but there are really two separate collections here. Chapters 25–7 contain a number of multiple-line sayings and have a high proportion of comparative sayings ('Like...is...') and imperatives; references to God are almost totally lacking. Chapters 28–9, on the other hand, strongly resemble the first Solomonic collection (10: 1–22: 16), with which they have a number of sayings in common.

25 MORE PROVERBS of Solomon transcribed by the men of Hezekiah king of Judah:

2   The glory of God is to keep things hidden
     but the glory of kings is to fathom them.
3   The heavens for height, the earth*a* for depth:

[a] Or the underworld.

unfathomable is the heart of a king.

Rid silver of its impurities,   4
then it may go to^a the silversmith;

rid the king's presence of wicked men,   5
and his throne will rest firmly on righteousness.

Do not put yourself forward in the king's presence   6
or take your place among the great;

for it is better that he should say to you, 'Come up 7
here',

than move you down to make room for a nobleman.

Be in no hurry to tell everyone what you have seen,   8
or it will end in bitter reproaches from your friend.

Argue your own case with your neighbour,   9
but do not reveal another man's secrets,

or he will reproach you when he hears of it   10
and your indiscretion will then be beyond recall.

Like apples of gold set in silver filigree   11
is a word spoken in season.

Like a golden earring or a necklace of Nubian gold   12
is a wise man whose reproof finds attentive ears.

Like the coolness of snow in harvest   13
is a trusty messenger to those who send him.^b

Like clouds and wind that bring no rain   14
is the man who boasts of gifts he never gives.

A prince may be persuaded by patience,   15
and a soft tongue may break down solid bone.^c

If you find honey, eat only what you need,   16
too much of it will make you sick;

be sparing in visits to your neighbour's house,   17
if he sees too much of you, he will dislike you.

[a] then it may go to: *or* and it will come out bright for.
[b] *Prob. rdg.; Heb. adds* refreshing his master.
[c] solid bone: *or* authority.

18 Like a club or a sword or a sharp arrow
    is a false witness who denounces his friend.

19 Like a tooth decayed or a foot limping
    is a traitor relied on in the day of trouble.

20 Like one who dresses*ᵃ* a wound with vinegar,
    so is the sweetest of singers to the heavy-hearted.

21 If your enemy is hungry, give him bread to eat;
    if he is thirsty, give him water to drink;

22 so you will heap glowing coals on his head,
    and the LORD will reward you.

23 As the north wind holds back the rain,
    so an angry glance holds back slander.

24 Better to live in a corner of the house-top
    than have a nagging wife and a brawling household.*ᵇ*

25 Like cold water to the throat when it is dry
    is good news from a distant land.

26 Like a muddied spring or a tainted well
    is a righteous man who gives way to a wicked one.

27 A surfeit of honey is bad for a man,
    and the quest for honour is burdensome.

28 Like a city that has burst out of its confining walls*ᶜ*
    is a man who cannot control his temper.

* 1. This heading provides valuable, though tantalizingly incomplete, information about the historical setting of Israelite wisdom literature and the composition of Proverbs. The reference to *the men of Hezekiah king of Judah* (about 715–687 B.C.), who were evidently scribes at the royal court, shows that wisdom literature, already associated with Solomon, was still a preoccupation of the Judaean court two centuries later.

[a] *Prob. rdg.; Heb. adds* a garment on a cold day.
[b] and a brawling household: *or, with slight change of consonants*, in a spacious house.
[c] *Or* that is breached and left unwalled.

It is unlikely that this scribal activity was confined to making fresh copies of old worn-out manuscripts. The meaning of the word translated by *transcribed* is uncertain, and something like 'edited' may be nearer the mark. But in any case it is highly probable that each new generation of court scribes would have made its own contribution to the royal library of wisdom books, either by preparing expanded editions of old books or by writing new ones.

2–7. A series of sayings about *kings*.

2. There appears to be no connection between the two halves of this verse apart from a verbal one, though each makes good sense by itself: mystery is of the essence of godhead, and a good king keeps his ear to the ground.

3. Once more a purely verbal connection (*fathom*, *unfathomable*) accounts for the juxtaposition of this saying and the previous one. The meaning is that it is as impossible to know the mind of a king as to measure the universe.

4–5. This four-line saying deals with the realities of politics. In recognizing that the mystique of royalty can in fact be penetrated and that kings' hearts are not really unfathomable it shows more realism than verse 3.

4. *then it may go to the silversmith*: the exact meaning of the Hebrew is uncertain, but the general sense is clear.

5. *will rest firmly on righteousness*: see the note on 20: 28.

6–7. Another four-line saying, this time in the Instruction form, about behaviour at court. This advice is in line with ancient Near Eastern wisdom literature generally. Jesus' parable about behaviour at a wedding feast (Luke 14: 8–11) probably alludes to this passage.

8. The N.E.B. translators take this saying as a general warning about gossip by altering the Hebrew, which has 'Be in no hurry to tell in court what you have seen'.

9–10. Here again it is not clear whether this is a private argument or a legal action. The point seems to be that even when the temptation is great – for example, when one is very anxious to win a case or an argument – it is foolish to reveal other people's confidences.

11–14. A series of comparisons. These little groups are characteristic of chapters 25–7.

11. *in season*: the meaning of the Hebrew phrase is not certain: it is not the same phrase as in 15: 23. But the saying is evidently concerned to point out the immense value to the speaker of the ability to use words skilfully.

12. *Nubian gold*: whether this is the real meaning is not certain; but other passages show that this was a type of gold which was highly prized.

13. The point of this saying is that the knowledge that he can rely on his messenger in a moment of crisis soothes a master's nerves as a cool drink would refresh a thirsty labourer working in the heat of harvest time (compare verse 25). *snow in harvest* would be a very rare phenomenon in Palestine. It may be that the author is thinking of snow brought especially down from the mountains or kept from the previous winter in an underground 'ice-hole'.

15. With the second line of this saying compare *Ahikar*, lines 105–6: 'Soft is the tongue of a king, but it breaks a dragon's ribs.'

16–17. Two sayings on the theme of moderation.

16. *find honey*: the reference is of course to wild honey. This is a proverb of wider application than the case cited: knowing when to stop eating honey is an example of moderation in general.

17. This saying is in the Instruction form. Compare *Ani*: 'Do not go freely to your neighbour's house, but enter it only when you are invited.'

20. Even after the omission of the intrusive line which the N.E.B. translators have relegated to a footnote, the meaning of this saying is still not clear. Perhaps the point is that even the best things can be harmful if used in inappropriate circumstances.

21–2. Compare 20: 22; 24: 17–18, 29 and *Counsels of Wisdom*, lines 41–4:

Do not return evil to the man who disputes with you;
requite with kindness your evil-doer,
maintain justice to your enemy,
smile on your adversary.

22. *heap glowing coals on his head*: presumably this is a
metaphor for embarrassment. The recipient of the unexpected
generosity will be overwhelmed by it and ashamed of himself
so that, as Paul wrote in his interpretation of this saying, the
person who confers it can be said to 'use good to defeat evil'
(Rom. 12: 20–1).

and the LORD will reward you: on the expectation of a reward see the note on 19: 17.

23. *holds back*: the usual translation of this word is 'gives
birth to'. But since in Palestine the north wind does not bring
rain, the N.E.B. translators have proposed another and
unusual meaning for the verb. If this is allowable, the saying
may mean that *an angry glance* at the right moment may serve
to prevent *slander* being uttered.

24. This saying is identical with 21: 9.

25. *from a distant land*: we are intended to picture a man
expecting news of crucial importance – perhaps commerical
or military – who has to wait weeks or months with growing
impatience and apprehension, not even knowing, in view of
the hazards of travel, when it will reach him. The relief when
the news arrives and proves to be good is overwhelming.

26. The uncertainty of the rainfall in Palestine gives a
special importance to every natural source of water, and the
contamination of a *spring* or *well* therefore fittingly symbolizes
the corruption of something good. The triumph of the
wicked man over the *righteous* comes under this heading in that
it is a reversal of the divinely established Order.

27. The first line of this saying may be compared with
verse 16; but the meaning of the second line is uncertain and
the point of the saying taken as a whole doubtful.

28. *control his temper*: the N.E.B. translation suggests a man

who is subject to outbursts of anger. This is not the meaning of the Hebrew, and 'control himself' would be a better translation. This is a more comprehensive concept, and corresponds exactly to the character of the ideal man of the ancient Near Eastern wisdom literature. The man who is unable to exercise self-control is as vulnerable as a city whose walls have been breached. ✶

26   Like snow in summer or rain at harvest,
       honour is unseasonable in a stupid man.

2   Like a fluttering sparrow or a darting swallow,
       groundless abuse gets nowhere.

3   The whip for a horse, the bridle for an ass,
       the rod for the back of a fool!

4   Do not answer a stupid man in the language of his
         folly,
       or you will grow like him;

5   answer a stupid man as his folly deserves,
       or he will think himself a wise man.

6   He who sends a fool on an errand
       cuts his own leg off and displays the stump.

7   A proverb in the mouth of stupid men
       dangles helpless as a lame man's legs.

8   Like one who gets the stone caught in his sling
       is he who bestows honour on a fool.

9   Like a thorn that pierces a drunkard's hand
       is a proverb in a stupid man's mouth.

10   Like an archer who shoots at any passer-by[a]
       is one who hires a stupid man or a drunkard.

11   Like a dog returning to its vomit
       is a stupid man who repeats his folly.

12   Do you see that man who thinks himself so wise?

[a] passer-by: *transposed from end of verse.*

There is more hope for a fool than for him.

The sluggard protests, 'There is a lion[a] in the highway,   13
a lion at large in the streets.'

A door turns on its hinges,   14
a sluggard on his bed.

A sluggard plunges his hand in the dish   15
but is too lazy to lift it to his mouth.

A sluggard is wiser in his own eyes   16
than seven men who answer sensibly.

Like a man who seizes a passing cur by the ears   17
is he who meddles[b] in another's quarrel.

A man who deceives another   19[c]
and then says, 'It was only a joke',
is like a madman shooting at random   18
his deadly darts and arrows.

For lack of fuel a fire dies down   20
and for want of a tale-bearer a quarrel subsides.

Like bellows[d] for the coal and fuel for the fire   21
is a quarrelsome man for kindling strife.

A gossip's whispers are savoury morsels   22
gulped down into the inner man.

Glib speech that covers a spiteful heart   23
is like glaze spread on earthenware.

With his lips an enemy may speak you fair   24
but inwardly he harbours deceit;
when his words are gracious, do not trust him,   25
for seven abominations fill his heart;
he may cloak his enmity in dissimulation,   26
but his wickedness is shown up before the assembly.

[a] *Or* snake.
[b] *So Vulg.; Heb.* is negligent *or* becomes enraged.
[c] *Verses 18 and 19 transposed.*
[d] *So Sept.; Heb.* coal.

27 If he digs a pit, he will fall into it;
    if he rolls a stone, it will roll back upon him.
28 A lying tongue makes innocence seem guilty,
    and smooth words conceal their sting.

* 1–12. These twelve sayings are all – with the exception of
verse 2 – about the *fool* or *stupid man* (the word is the same in
Hebrew).

1. *is unseasonable*: literally, 'unfitting'.

2. *abuse*: literally, 'curse'. Blessings and curses were believed in the ancient Semitic world to be in themselves the
effective agency of the wish which they expressed. This saying
introduces a qualification to this belief: curses are only effective when they are deserved; if they are *groundless* they fly
harmlessly by the person for whom they are intended, like a
bird.

4–5. In the Hebrew the contrast between these two sayings
is even more striking than in the English translation: their
first lines are exactly identical apart from the negative *Do not*
of verse 4. These two apparently contradictory sayings have
been placed together to show that human problems are often
complicated and cannot always be solved by an appeal to a
simple universal rule. This observation marks a significant
step in the development of human thought.

6. The meaning of this saying is clear apart from the last
three words: to send a man *on an errand* is to provide oneself
temporarily with an extra pair of legs. But if the messenger is a
fool, the effect is disastrous. But the meaning of the words translated *and displays the stump* is uncertain.

8. *gets the stone caught*: literally, 'wraps up'. Only someone
who did not know how a sling functions could do such a
stupid thing. The point is that to bestow *honour on a fool* is to
misuse it. Compare verse 1.

9. *is a proverb in a stupid man's mouth*: in the Hebrew this
line is exactly identical with the first line of verse 7. The

similarity between the two sayings is clearer in the Hebrew, because there in both cases it forms the second line. The point is that the *stupid man* cannot even be trusted with a piece of good advice, but will inevitably misapply it and so do himself harm.

10. This verse is very difficult. If the N.E.B. translation is correct it is a warning against hiring people without adequate references: such folly may injure other people as well.

11. The point of this saying is that the *stupid man* never learns from his experiences. He can thus be compared to a *dog*, which is so lacking in discrimination that it eats its own *vomit*.

13–16. A collection of sayings, mainly humorous, about the *sluggard* or lazy man.

13. See the note on 22: 13.

14. There is more than one kind of movement: the *sluggard* chooses that of the *door*, which moves without going anywhere!

15. See the note on 19: 24.

16. *seven men*: an indefinite number. The purpose of the saying is to point out that constitutionally lazy people are often self-satisfied.

17. *meddles*: the Hebrew may mean 'becomes enraged' or 'gets excited'.

18–19. The transposition of the two verses in this saying (see the footnote) does not in this case imply that the N.E.B. translators believe that the Hebrew text is in disorder, but has been made simply for the sake of English style. The point is that certain kinds of practical joke can have serious social consequences.

20–8. A group of sayings about malicious speech.

21. *bellows*: this translation is based on an alteration of the Hebrew text, which has a word meaning 'coal' or 'charcoal'. The footnote claims that the N.E.B. translation follows the Septuagint; but this is not the case: the Septuagint has a word meaning 'hearth'. It is quite possible that the Hebrew is correct: piling on more fuel keeps a fire going.

22. This verse is identical with 18 : 8, on which see the note.

24–7. The N.E.B. takes these four verses as constituting a single saying; in other translations verse 27 is rendered as a separate saying.

24. An alternative translation of the first line would be 'A man full of hatred disguises it with his words'.

25. *seven*: see the note on verse 16.

26. *the assembly*: the word is the same as that translated by 'public assembly' in 5 : 14. It can have the meaning of a religious meeting, but here it probably means an informal gathering of citizens, in which reputations could be made or destroyed.

28. This verse is difficult, and the N.E.B. translation represents only one of a number of attempts to make sense of it.

conceal their sting: the Hebrew has 'bring about destruction'. ✳

27 Do not flatter yourself about tomorrow,
    for you never know what a day will bring forth.
2   Let flattery come from a stranger, not from yourself,
    from the lips of an outsider and not from your own.
3   Stone is a burden and sand a dead weight,
    but to be vexed by a fool is more burdensome than either.
4   Wrath is cruel and anger is a deluge;
    but who can stand up to jealousy?
5   Open reproof is better
    than love concealed.
6   The blows a friend gives are well meant,
    but the kisses of an enemy are perfidious.[a]
7   A man full-fed refuses honey,
    but even bitter food tastes sweet to a hungry man.
8   Like a bird that strays far from its nest

[a] *Mng. of Heb. word uncertain.*

is a man far from his home.

Oil and perfume bring joy to the heart,   9
but cares torment a man's very soul.[a]

Do not neglect your own friend or your father's;[b]   10
a neighbour at hand is better than a brother far away.

Be wise, my son, then you will bring joy to my heart, 11
and I shall be able to forestall my critics.

A shrewd man sees trouble coming and lies low;   12
the simple walk into it and pay the penalty.

Take a man's garment when he pledges his word for 13
   a stranger
and hold that as a pledge for the unknown person.

If one man greets another too heartily,[c]   14
he may give great offence.

Endless dripping on a rainy day –   15
that is what a nagging wife is like.

As well try to control the wind as to control her!   16
As well try to pick up oil in one's fingers!

As iron sharpens iron,   17
so one man sharpens the wits[d] of another.

He who guards the fig-tree will eat its fruit,   18
and he who watches his master's interests will come to
   honour.

As face answers face reflected in the water,   19
so one man's heart answers another's.

Sheol and Abaddon are insatiable;   20
a man's eyes too are never satisfied.

The melting-pot is for silver and the crucible for gold, 21

[a] but cares...soul: *so Sept.; Heb.* but friendship is sweeter than one's
own counsel.
[b] *Prob. rdg.; Heb. adds* or how should you enter your brother's house
in the day of your ruin?
[c] *So one MS.; others add* rising early in the morning.
[d] *Lit.* face.

but praise is the test of character.

22 Pound a fool with pestle and mortar,[a]
his folly will never be knocked out of him.

23 Be careful to know your own sheep
and take good care of your flocks;

24 for possessions do not last for ever,
nor will a crown endure to endless generations.

25 The grass disappears, new shoots are seen
and the green growth on the hills is gathered in;

26 the lambs clothe you,
the he-goats are worth the price of a field,

27 while the goats' milk is enough for your food[b]
and nourishment for your maidens.

⋆ 1. Compare *Amen-em-opet* XVIII 19: 13: 'Man does not know what the morrow will be like.'

5. The point of this saying is not clear. 'Pretended love' would give a somewhat better contrast than *love concealed*, but the Hebrew will not bear this meaning.

6. *The blows a friend gives* are the unpalatable home truths which may wound his friend, but which are needed to bring him to his senses and to prevent him from doing something wrong or foolish. This line in its older English translation ('Faithful are the wounds of a friend') has become a familiar saying in English.

the kisses of an enemy: such as the kiss with which Judas Iscariot betrayed Jesus.

7. The point of this saying seems to be that human reactions are subjective and governed by circumstances. Compare *Ahikar*, line 188: 'Hunger sweetens that which is bitter.'

refuses: the Hebrew word means 'tramples on'.

8. Community ties were very strong in the societies of the

[a] *Prob. rdg.; Heb. adds* with groats.
[b] *Prob. rdg., cp. Sept.; Heb. adds* for your household's food.

ancient Near East, and the individual who was cut off from his own community was regarded as lost and helpless. Compare *Papyrus Insinger* XXII 28: 24: 'When the wise man is abroad, his heart sighs after his native land.'

9. The Hebrew of the second line of this saying is difficult, and none of the attempts to correct it has been entirely convincing.

10. The Hebrew text of this saying has three lines (see the N.E.B. footnote), and one is probably not original. The N.E.B. translators omit the second line; but the other two still do not make a very satisfactory saying.

11. The point of this saying, which is in the Instruction form and resembles the introductions to the Instructions in chapters 1–9, is that the reputation of the teacher depends on the extent to which his pupils have profited from his instruction.

12. This saying is virtually identical with 22: 3.

13. This saying is virtually identical with 20: 16, on which see the note.

14. The Hebrew has 'The man who blesses another with a loud voice, rising early in the morning, will be treated as a curse'. This may simply be concerned with good manners, or, if we take the words 'bless' and 'curse' literally, with the insincerity which is often concealed behind a hearty manner. The words 'rising early in the morning', though found in virtually all the Hebrew manuscripts (see the footnote), are probably a rather trivial addition by a later copyist.

15–16. The N.E.B. translation implies that these verses form a single continuous saying, and this is probably so, although the meaning of verse 16 is difficult, and the rendering of the N.E.B. is a paraphrase rather than a translation. The first line of verse 15 is similar to the second line of 19: 13.

17. *wits*: literally, 'face'. This Hebrew word is used in several metaphorical senses including 'self', but the meaning 'wits' is not found elsewhere. Nevertheless the context seems to require some such meaning here: the word *sharpens*, used

of human beings, most naturally refers to the intellect. If this is the correct interpretation, the saying is a plea for the importance of intellectual conversation such as was presumably to be found in the wisdom school and also probably at the informal meetings at the city gate.

19. The second line of this saying is, literally, 'so (is) the heart of a man to a man'. The N.E.B. translators have interpreted this as referring to two different men; if this is correct, it might mean that one understands one's own character through observing that of others. Alternatively the meaning may be that a man sees himself in his own heart: that is, he reaches an understanding of himself through self-examination; or again it could mean that the character (*heart*) of a man is reflected in the man himself, that is, in his actions.

20. *Sheol and Abaddon*: see the note on 15: 11. Here, as in 1: 12 (on which see the note), it is the insatiability of Sheol which is made the point of comparison with *a man's eyes*, that is, his desires and ambitions.

21. The first line of this saying refers to the need to assay or test the purity of metals, and the second asserts that human *character* similarly needs to be tested, and that in this case the best method is to enquire about a man's reputation (N.E.B. *praise*). If he has a good reputation he can be trusted.

22. This saying is even more pessimistic about the incorrigibility of the *fool* than 26: 3.

23–7. These verses constitute a single unit in the form of an Instruction (verse 23) followed by a reasoned argument. The purpose seems to be to commend the pastoral life as the only satisfactory and enduring means of livelihood. This theme appears somewhat strange in a book mainly addressed to the courtiers of Jerusalem, but the dichotomy between town and country was not then as sharp as it is now: note, for example, how Absalom, the son of king David, attended to his sheep-farms (2 Sam. 13: 23). The courtier, who would no doubt normally possess similar ancestral estates in the country, is here warned that in the long run these will serve him in better stead than the glittering but ephemeral prizes to be won at court, or through trade, which was mainly in the hands of those active in government.

24. *possessions*: the word refers to accumulated wealth.

a crown: this word is not elsewhere used metaphorically, but always referred, during the period of the Israelite monarchy, to the king's own crown. This section can hardly be addressed to the king or to a royal prince, as were some wisdom books, since the statement *nor will a crown endure to endless generations* flatly contradicts the firmly held belief that the Judaean dynasty of descendants of David would last for ever. Because of this difficulty it has been suggested that the word *crown* is a mistake for a similar word meaning 'treasure'. ✳

The wicked man runs away with no one in pursuit, **28**
but the righteous is like a young lion in repose.

It is the fault of a violent man[a] that quarrels start,[b]   2
but they are settled[c] by a man of discernment.

A tyrant oppressing the poor   3
is like driving rain which ruins the crop.

The lawless praise wicked men;   4
the law-abiding contend with them.

Bad men do not know what justice is,   5
but those who seek the LORD know everything good.[d]

Better be poor and above reproach   6
than rich and crooked.

A discerning son observes the law,   7
but one who keeps riotous company wounds his father.

He who grows rich by lending at discount or at interest   8
is saving for another who will be generous to the poor.

[a] violent man: *so Sept.; Heb.* land.
[b] start: *prob. rdg., cp. Sept.; Heb.* her officers.
[c] they are settled: *so Sept.; Heb.* a knowing man thus prolongs.
[d] good: *so Targ.; Heb. om.*

9   If a man turns a deaf ear to the law,
    even his prayers are an abomination.

10 He who tempts the upright into evil courses
    will himself fall into the pit he has dug.
    The honest shall inherit a fortune,
    but the wicked shall inherit nothing.[a]

11 The rich man may think himself wise,
    but a poor man of discernment sees through him.

12 When the just are in power, there are great celebrations,[b]
    but when the wicked come to the top, others are
        downtrodden.

13 Conceal your faults, and you will not prosper;
    confess and give them up, and you will find mercy.

14 Happy the man who is scrupulous in conduct,
    but he who hardens his heart falls into misfortune.

15 Like a starving lion or a thirsty bear
    is a wicked man ruling a helpless people.

16 The man who is stupid and grasping will perish,
    but he who hates ill-gotten gain will live long.

17 A man charged with bloodshed
    will jump into a well to escape arrest.

18 Whoever leads an honest life will be safe,
    but a rogue will fail, one way or another.

19 One who cultivates his land has plenty to eat;
    idle pursuits lead to poverty.

20 A man of steady character will enjoy many blessings,
    but one in a hurry to grow rich will not go unpunished.

21 To show favour is not good;
    but men will do wrong for a mere crust of bread.

22 The miser[c] is in a hurry to grow rich,

[a] but...nothing: *prob. rdg.*, *cp. Sept.*; *Heb. om.*
[b] *Or* there is great pageantry.
[c] *Or* The man with the evil eye.

never dreaming that want will overtake him.

Take a man to task and in the end[a] win more thanks 23
than the man with a flattering tongue.

To rob your father or mother and say you do no wrong 24
is no better than wanton destruction.

A self-important[b] man provokes quarrels, 25
but he who trusts in the LORD grows fat and prosperous.

It is plain stupidity to trust in one's own wits, 26
but he who walks the path of wisdom will come safely
    through.

He who gives to the poor will never want, 27
but he who turns a blind eye gets nothing but curses.

When the wicked come to the top, others are pulled 28
    down;[c]
but, when they perish, the righteous come into power.

✶ 1. *is like a young lion in repose*: an alternative translation
would be 'has the confidence of a young lion'. *The wicked
man* is punished by his guilty conscience, while the *righteous*
man's reward is his clear conscience, which enables him to sail
confidently through life.

2. The Hebrew of this verse is very difficult, and the N.E.B.
translators have mainly followed the Septuagint, which has a
quite different text. A reasonable sense can, however, be obtained from the Hebrew of the first line: 'When a land rebels,
its leaders are many.' This might mean that a rebellious people
is punished by the horrors of a civil war between many rival
claimants for the throne. But the Hebrew of the second line is
virtually untranslatable, and the Septuagint variant is probably
preferable for the whole verse.

3. *A tyrant*: the Hebrew has 'a poor man'; but the idea of
a poor man oppressing the poor is an unlikely one, and the

[a] in the end: *so one MS.; others have an obscure form.*
[b] *Or* grasping.
[c] are pulled down: *or* hide themselves.

N.E.B. is probably right in supposing that a letter has been accidentally lost, changing an original 'tyrant' into a 'poor man'.

4. *lawless...law-abiding*: literally, 'those who forsake the law...those who keep the law'. During the last few centuries before Christ the word 'law' (Hebrew *Torah*) became a technical term meaning the will of God embodied in the Pentateuch, which was regarded by all Jews as the foundation of their religious faith and life. It has been suggested that it has this meaning here; but elsewhere in Proverbs it is used of the teaching of the wisdom teachers, and this is probably its meaning here also. The saying asserts that the wisdom teaching is on the side of morality.

5. *everything good*: the Hebrew simply has 'everything': that is, true followers of Yahweh (*those who seek the LORD*) are, as is said in John 16: 13 of the work of the Holy Spirit, guided 'into all the truth'. Wickedness is here regarded as associated with spiritual blindness.

6. This saying is a variant of 19: 1.

7. *the law*: see the note on verse 4.

8. *lending at discount or at interest*: both are strictly forbidden in Lev. 25: 36 and condemned elsewhere in the Old Testament. The technical difference between *discount* and *interest* is explained in the N.E.B. translation of Lev. 25: 36, where these two words are rendered by 'deducting it (the interest) in advance from the capital sum' and 'adding it on repayment'.

another: that is, his heir. As 13: 22 points out, 'the sinner's hoard passes to the righteous'. The saying takes it for granted that lending at interest is wrong, but affirms that in the long run the divinely established Order will prevail, and evil be overcome by good.

9. *the law*: there is a case in this religious context for taking this to mean the Law of Moses here; but probably, as in verses 4 and 7, it refers to the wisdom teaching.

abomination: see the note on 3: 32, and compare *Ptah-hotep*: 'He whom God loves is a hearer, but he whom God hates cannot hear', where 'hear' is a technical term for conformity to the teaching.

10. In the Hebrew this verse has only three lines. The third fits quite well with the first two, but in view of the fact that three-line sayings are very rare, the N.E.B. translators have made up a fourth line on the basis of a hint in the Septuagint, so producing two two-line sayings.

11. It is not stated in this saying that the conceited *rich man* will actually lose his wealth to the *poor man of discernment*, but this is perhaps implied, and would be in keeping with the principle expressed elsewhere that wisdom is bound to succeed and pride to fall.

12. This saying appears to make a rather obvious comment on the results of good and evil rule, though there are signs that the original meaning may have been obscured by mistakes in the copying of the text.

are in power: the Hebrew has 'rejoice'; the N.E.B. translators have altered the text to produce better sense.

are downtrodden: the verb normally means 'sought out', and so might mean 'hunted down' here. This would give reasonable sense, but the N.E.B. translators have postulated the existence of another verb with the same spelling meaning 'trample, tread down'.

13. This saying, which is unique in Proverbs, stresses the necessity of the confession of sins and expresses confidence that God is merciful. The confession of sins was widely practised in the ancient Near East, and there we occasionally find a belief in divine mercy somewhat comparable to the teaching of the Old Testament, e.g. in an Egyptian prayer from an ancient tombstone:

Although the servant has been disposed to do evil,
Yet is the Lord disposed to be merciful.
The Lord of Thebes (the god Amon) does not remain
    angry for a whole day:
his anger is finished in a moment, and nothing is left.

Nevertheless, these beliefs are much more prominent in the Old Testament, and this saying, although it does not actually mention God, probably reflects Israelite beliefs.

14. *scrupulous in conduct*: the Hebrew has 'who fears continually', and the same expression in Ecclus. 37: 12 is rendered 'godfearing' in the N.E.B. Apocrypha. This gives a quite different sense to the saying.

15. *starving...thirsty*: the normal meaning of these words is 'roaring' and 'charging'; and the N.E.B. translators themselves so render the former word in connection with a lion in Isa. 5: 29–30.

16. *will perish*: the Hebrew has no verb here, but a noun: 'a ruler who is stupid is an oppressor'. This does not make good sense, and the N.E.B. translators have tried to make sense by assuming that the word 'ruler' is a mistake for a verb meaning *perish*, which gives a good contrast with *will live long*.

17. The N.E.B. translation of this verse is based on a radical rewriting of a Hebrew text which makes very little sense: 'A man who is burdened with another person's blood will flee to a pit: do not seize him.' The whole verse is in prose rather than poetry, and may have found its way into Proverbs by accident.

18. *one way or another*: literally, 'by one'. Some commentators, unconvinced that the Hebrew text can be made to yield a satisfactory sense, think that this word is a mistake for another which means 'into a pit'.

19. This verse is similar to 12: 11.

idle pursuits lead to poverty: the Hebrew, literally 'he who pursues worthless things will have plenty of poverty', brings out the contrast more effectively.

20–2. Three sayings on the evils of the love of money.

20. This saying is about getting one's priorities right.

steady character: literally, 'faithfulness' – the man who puts his responsibilities to others first will in fact end up comfortably off (literally, *enjoy many blessings*), whereas the man who puts his ambition and greed before everything else is an enemy of society and so will inevitably fail in his ambitions and come to a bad end.

21. This saying is concerned with the accepting of bribes by judges.

22. Compare verse 20.

23. Compare 27: 6 on the need for plain speaking.

24. *wanton destruction*: the N.E.B. is vague here. The Hebrew says that this kind of person is 'companion to a destroyer'. *To rob* and yet to *say you do no wrong* suggests the swindling of aged parents by some shady deal regarding the family property which is just within the law; and the point seems to be that such an action is a hardly less heinous crime than murdering one's parents.

25–6. Two sayings about selfishness and pride.

25. *self-important*: the footnote gives an alternative translation: 'grasping'. The Hebrew is capable of both meanings: literally, either 'wide of soul' or 'wide of appetite'. Either kind of man might be said to provoke *quarrels*, and could be contrasted with the man who *trusts in the LORD*, that is, who is humble and not self-seeking.

26. The point of this saying is the same as that of verse 25 except that the religious element is missing.

28. Compare verse 12.

pulled down: the alternative translation given in the N.E.B. footnote is the normal one, and makes good sense. ✳

A man who is still stubborn after much reproof　　**29**
will suddenly be broken past mending.
When the righteous are in power the people rejoice,　2
but they groan when the wicked hold office.
A lover of wisdom brings joy to his father,　　　3
but one who keeps company with harlots squanders
　　his wealth.
By just government a king gives his country stability, 4
but by forced contributions he reduces it to ruin.

5 A man who flatters his neighbour
is spreading a net for his feet.

6 An evil man is ensnared by his sin,*a*
but a righteous man lives*b* and flourishes.

7 The righteous man is concerned for the cause of the
helpless,
but the wicked understand no such concern.

8 Arrogance can inflame a city,
but wisdom averts the people's anger.

9 If a wise man goes to law with a fool,
he will meet abuse or derision, but get no remedy.

10 Men who have tasted blood hate an honest man,
but the upright set much store by his life.

11 A stupid man gives free rein to his anger;
a wise man waits and lets it grow cool.

12 If a prince listens to falsehood,
all his servants will be wicked.

13 Poor man and oppressor have this in common:
what happiness each has comes from the LORD.*c*

14 A king who steadfastly deals out justice to the weak
will be secure for ever on his throne.

15 Rod and reprimand impart wisdom,
but a boy who runs wild brings shame on his mother.

16 When the wicked are in power, sin is in power,
but the righteous will gloat over their downfall.

17 Correct your son, and he will be a comfort to you
and bring you delights of every kind.

18 Where there is no one in authority,*d* the people break
loose,

[a] An evil...sin: *or* When an evil man steps out a trap awaits him.
[b] lives: *so some MSS.; others obscure.*
[c] what...LORD: *lit.* the LORD makes the eyes of both of them
shine.
[d] *Or* no vision.

but a guardian of the law keeps them on the straight
    path.

Mere words will not keep a slave in order;   19
he may understand, but he will not respond.

When you see someone over-eager to speak,[a]   20
there will be more hope for a fool than for him.

Pamper a slave from boyhood,   21
and in the end he will prove ungrateful.

A man prone to anger provokes a quarrel   22
and a hot-head is always doing wrong.

Pride will bring a man low;   23
a man lowly in spirit wins honour.

He who goes shares with a thief is his own enemy: 24
he hears himself put on oath and dare not give evidence.

A man's fears will prove a snare to him,   25
but he who trusts in the LORD has a high tower of
    refuge.

Many seek audience of a prince,   26
but in every case the LORD decides.

The righteous cannot abide an unjust man,   27
nor the wicked a man whose conduct is upright.

---

* 1. *is still stubborn*: literally, 'hardens his neck'. The metaphor is similar to that in the fable of the oak and the bulrush:
the pliant bulrush survives the storm because it bends to the
wind, while the rigid oak, though strong enough to resist a
good deal of buffeting, *will suddenly be broken past mending*
when the real storm comes.

2. Compare 28: 12, 28.

3. The fate of the man *who keeps company with harlots* is
dealt with at length in chapters 1–9. Both there and here
(compare especially 5: 10; 6: 31) the financial consequences
are especially stressed. This may seem an unduly mercenary

[a] *Or* someone hasty in business.

attitude, but it should be remembered that wealth was regarded as a sign of divine blessing and was an essential factor in establishing a family's honourable standing in the community. To squander it was therefore not only an act of personal folly but also a betrayal of the family and its head.

4. *forced contributions*: the right of kings to exact taxes was universally recognized. But kings were tempted to tax their people beyond a reasonable limit, often for the sake of an ambition to erect magnificent buildings or to undertake unnecessary wars of conquest. From the time of Solomon onwards Israelites suffered such treatment from a number of their rulers. Compare Samuel's description of life under a monarchy in 1 Sam. 8: 11–18.

6. The first line of this saying is rather cryptic in the Hebrew, but the general sense is clear whether we accept the text of the N.E.B. or the footnote, which is based on two slight alterations of the text.

7. *the cause of the helpless* was an especial concern of some of the Old Testament prophets, but a similar concern is found in the laws and wisdom literature of the ancient Near East.

8. Compare 11: 10, 11; 12: 20 on the relationship between the individual and the community.

9. Like 26: 4, this saying affirms that no kind of reasonable activity can be carried on with a *fool*: it is better to cut one's losses and have nothing further to do with him.

but get no remedy: literally, 'and there is no quietness'. This may mean either that the matter will never be satisfactorily settled or that the fool will pour out a never-ending stream of *abuse* and *derision* in court.

10. *Men who have tasted blood*: literally, 'men of blood', that is, violent men or murderers. The *honest man* stands in their way, and therefore they *hate* him; but that is the very reason why the *upright* citizens respect him.

set much store by: this translation is based on a slight alteration of the text. The Hebrew has 'seek his life', which usually means 'seek to kill' rather than 'honour'.

11. Compare such sayings as 16: 32; 25: 28.

12. This saying offers direct advice on the duties of a king, and should be understood in the light of other sayings on the same subject. A king has been divinely endowed with the ability to discover the truth of what he is told (compare 16: 10; 20: 8), and he must do so (compare 25: 2). The writer also has a sense of political reality and knows that weak régimes are also usually corrupt.

13. See the note on 22: 2.

14. *will be secure for ever on his throne*: compare 16: 12; 20: 28; 25: 5.

15. Compare 13: 24; 23: 13–14 and see the notes on those verses.

16. Compare 28: 12, 28; 29: 2.

18. The N.E.B. translation depends on unusual translations of several words. If these are given their usual sense the meaning is quite different:

> Where there is no prophetic vision, the people break loose, but the man who observes the law will be blessed.

19. A simple piece of practical advice: only corporal punishment will cure dumb insolence.

24. *hears himself put on oath*: literally, 'hears the curse'. The reference is probably to a law such as Lev. 5: 1, which makes refusal to give evidence a crime. The divine authority behind such a law would make it tantamount to a curse on those who disobeyed it (compare Judg. 17: 2).

is his own enemy: literally, 'hates his own life'. In view of what has been said above, this may mean not merely that such a person does harm to himself but that he will henceforward wish he was dead, since he will be afraid that the curse may have its effect at any moment.

25. *A man's fears*: the Hebrew has 'the fear of a man'. This can be taken either as the N.E.B. translators have taken it, or as meaning 'being afraid of (other) men'. In either case the contrast is between the deleterious effects of letting fear guide

one's life and that release from fear which comes from putting one's trust in God.

26. *audience*: literally, 'the face'. The first line of this saying by itself might refer either to courtiers trying to obtain advancement by means of a private audience with the king, or to litigants seeking a decision from him as appeal judge. The use of the word translated *case* (literally, 'judgement') makes the second interpretation the more probable one. In other words, behind the king's judicial decision lies that of the highest court of all: God.

27. *cannot abide*: literally, 'abominates' – a very strong expression elsewhere used of God's loathing of wickedness: see 3: 32. ✳

SECTION VI. PROVERBS 30: 1-33

THE SAYINGS OF AGUR

30 Sayings of Agur son of Jakeh from Massa: [a]

This is the great man's very word: I am weary, O God,
I am weary and worn out;

2 I am a dumb brute, scarcely a man,
without a man's powers of understanding;

3 I have not learnt wisdom
nor have I received knowledge from the Holy One.

4 Who has ever gone up to heaven and come down again?
Who has cupped the wind in the hollow of his hands?
Who has bound up the waters in the fold of his
garment?
Who has fixed the boundaries of the earth?
What is his name or his son's name, if you know it?

[a] from Massa: *prob. rdg.* (*cp.* 31: 1); *Heb.* the oracle.

God's every promise has stood the test: 5
he is a shield to all who seek refuge with him.
Add nothing to his words,   6
or he will expose you for a liar.
Two things I ask of thee;   7
do not withhold them from me before I die.
Put fraud and lying far from me;   8
give me neither poverty nor wealth,
provide me only with the food I need.
If I have too much, I shall deny thee   9
and say, 'Who is the LORD?'
If I am reduced to poverty, I shall steal
and blacken the name of my God.

Never disparage a slave to his master,   10
or he will speak ill of you, and you will pay for it.
There is a sort of people who defame their fathers   11
and do not speak well of their own mothers;
a sort who are pure in their own eyes   12
and yet are not cleansed of their filth;
a sort – how haughty are their looks,   13
how disdainful their glances!
A sort whose teeth are swords,   14
their jaws are set with knives,
they eat the wretched out of the country
and the needy out of house and home.[a]

* Chapter 30 is headed *Sayings of Agur son of Jakeh from Massa*. Although the next heading does not occur until 31:1, the diversity of the material in chapter 30 suggests that the heading applies only to part of it. This hypothesis is supported by the different arrangement of the material in the Septuagint,

[a] house and home: *prob. rdg.; Heb.* man.

which divides the chapter into two, placing verses 1–14 after 22: 17–24: 22 and verses 15–33 after 24: 34. In fact the original *Sayings of Agur* may not have extended beyond the first three, or possibly four, verses; the remainder was added to them, eventually forming a collection of fourteen verses, before this was in turn combined with other collections.

1–3. Except for the heading, the Hebrew of verse 1 is unintelligible (see the note on verse 1), but in its original form it probably contained the beginning of the confession attributed to Agur of which verses 2–3 are the continuation.

1. *Agur son of Jakeh*: neither of these names occurs elsewhere in the Old Testament, and their form makes it unlikely that they are Israelite names. These verses are consequently non-Israelite wisdom literature, presumably taken over by the Israelite wise men at an early date.

from Massa: the Hebrew simply has the single word 'Massa'. The same word occurs in the heading to the Sayings of Lemuel in 31: 1, where it poses the same problem. It could be a Hebrew word meaning a prophetic oracle (see the N.E.B. footnote), and it has sometimes been so translated. But the verses which follow are not an oracle, and it is more probable that it is a proper name designating the place or region where Agur lived. Since Massa is given as the name of a 'son' of the desert-dweller Ishmael in Gen. 25: 14 and 1 Chron. 1: 30, it may have been a tribe or district of north Arabia.

The remainder of this verse is obscure. The Hebrew seems to read 'The saying of the man to Ithiel, to Ithiel and Ucal'. These names are not only unknown, but unlikely; moreover the Septuagint had a text in which they did not occur. Various attempts have been made to reconstruct the original Hebrew text which has suffered corruption; the N.E.B. translation is one of a number, all of which are very speculative.

This is the great man's very word: the Hebrew has simply 'saying of the man'!

2–3. This confession of Agur that his intelligence, when compared with God's *wisdom*, puts him on the level of the *dumb brute*, is reminiscent of other passages in the Old Testament such as Ps. 49: 10–12; 73: 21–2.

4. The activities referred to in these rhetorical questions are things which only God can do, and the point of the questions, ending with the ironical *if you know it*, is to emphasize the absurdity of man's comparing himself with God or claiming to be independent of him. There is a similar and much longer series of such questions in Job 38–41, where it is God who speaks. Here, however, there is no reason to suppose that the questions are attributed to God. The verse may be a continuation of verses 2–3, but this is not certain. Much of the language used to describe the various acts of creation is derived from traditional sources: compare Job 38: 4–5; Isa. 40: 12.

5–9. It is not certain whether these verses originally formed a single unit. Verses 5–6 are a statement affirming the reliability and sufficiency of God's word (translated *promise* in the N.E.B.) and the danger of tampering with it, while verses 7–9 are a prayer.

5–6. Verse 5 is identical, apart from some small details, with part of Ps. 18: 30, the first line of verse 6 is similar to a phrase in Deut. 4: 2, and its second line is reminiscent of Job 13: 10; 24: 25 *b* (in the Hebrew, 'make me a liar'). This suggests that these two verses were composed after Israelite wisdom teaching had become integrated with that of Judaism: it was characteristic of this late wisdom (for example, Ecclesiasticus, written in the second century B.C.) to quote older biblical books and also to insist on the reliability, sufficiency and sacred character of God's word or Law enshrined in the Scriptures.

7–9. These verses also express a type of piety characteristic of a period when wisdom literature had become primarily a means of expressing certain aspects of the Jewish faith. The two requests, of which the second is expressed at greater length than the first, are not for material things but for divine help in providing the petitioner with the moral character and outward circumstances of life which will enable him to maintain his religious faith and an honest way of life in accordance with God's will.

10. This two-line saying is unrelated to the rest of the chapter. The precise bearing of the second line on the first is not clear.

speak ill of you: literally, 'curse you'. On the power of the curse see the note on 26: 2.

11–14. This is a collection of four sayings, each beginning in the Hebrew with the same word, *a sort*. They probably belong to the class of 'numerical sayings' (on which see the note on 6: 16–19) of which several other examples occur in this chapter. The only difference is that this collection lacks the introductory formula (e.g., in verse 15, *Three...four*). Possibly there was originally a similar formula here which has been lost.

11. *defame*: literally, 'curse'; *speak well of*: literally, 'bless'. On the sin of cursing parents see the note on 20: 20.

14. a four-line saying.

out of house and home: the Hebrew has 'from among men'. The N.E.B. translation, which is based on a slight change of the text which yields a word meaning 'agricultural land' or 'landed property', makes a better parallel with *the country*. ✳

A COLLECTION OF NUMERICAL SAYINGS

15 The leech has two daughters;
'Give', says one, and 'Give', says the other.

Three things there are which will never be satisfied,
four which never say, 'Enough!'

16 The grave*a* and a barren womb,*b*
a land thirsty for water
and fire that never says, 'Enough!'

[a] *Heb.* Sheol.
[b] *Or* a woman's desire.

The eye that mocks a father or scorns a mother's old 17
    age[a]
will be plucked out by magpies
or eaten by the vulture's young.

Three things there are which are too wonderful for me, 18
    four which I do not understand:
    the way of a vulture in the sky, 19
    the way of a serpent on the rock,
    the way of a ship out at sea,
    and the way of a man with a girl.

The way of an unfaithful wife is this: 20
    she eats, then she wipes her mouth
    and says, 'I have done no harm.'

At three things the earth shakes, 21
    four things it cannot bear:
    a slave turned king, 22
    a churl gorging himself,
    a woman unloved when she is married, 23
    and a slave-girl displacing her mistress.

Four things there are which are smallest on earth 24
    yet wise beyond the wisest:
    ants, a people with no strength, 25
    yet they prepare their store of food in the summer;
    rock-badgers, a feeble folk, 26
    yet they make their home among the rocks;
    locusts, which have no king, 27
    yet they all sally forth in detachments;[b]
    the lizard, which can be grasped in the hand, 28
    yet is found in the palaces of kings.

[a] old age: *prob. rdg.; Heb. unintelligible.*
[b] *Mng. of Heb. word uncertain.*

29 Three things there are which are stately in their stride,
   four which are stately as they move:
30   the lion, a hero among beasts,
     which will not turn tail for anyone;
31   the strutting cock*a* and the he-goat;
     and a king going forth to lead his army.*b*

32   If you are churlish and arrogant
     and fond of filthy talk, hold your tongue;
33   for wringing out the milk produces curd
     and wringing the nose produces blood,
     so provocation*c* leads to strife.

✻ This section consists of five numerical sayings (see the note on 6: 16–19), to which a few other sayings have been added.

15*a*. The first two lines of this verse stand by themselves. They were probably placed here because of their similarity of theme with the numerical saying which follows. But the meaning is not entirely clear. The word translated *leech* is similar to the name of a demon in Arabian folklore, but the N.E.B. translation is probably correct: this is the bloodsucking little creature known as the *leech*, and the *daughters* may be its two suckers. But the second line is cryptic: in the Hebrew it consists simply of two monosyllables, which may be translated 'Give! give!' There may be something missing from the text; but if the interpretation of the N.E.B. is correct, the saying may be intended as a comment on human avarice which, like the leech, is never satisfied. This interpretation might account for this saying's having been placed in proximity to the saying in verse 15*b* on the *things...which will never be satisfied*.

15*b*-16. These verses are simply based on observation of

[a] strutting cock: *or* charger; *mng. of Heb. uncertain.*
[b] going forth to lead his army: *prob. rdg.; Heb. unintelligible.*
[c] provocation: *lit.* wringing the nostrils.

life. On the insatiability of the *grave* (see the N.E.B. footnote) see the note on 1:12. The alternative translation to *barren womb* in the N.E.B. fits the context equally well.

17. This saying is unrelated to its context, though its theme is similar to that of verse 11. Since the son's contempt for his parents has been conveyed in his scornful look, it is appropriately his *eye* which will be plucked out. Presumably it is envisaged that the offender will die in a desolate place and so will suffer the terrible fate of not being buried. See the notes on 20:20.

magpies: the Hebrew has 'ravens of the river-valley'.

18–19. This saying is, perhaps intentionally, open to a number of interpretations. What – apart from the word *way* – is the common element? Neither the theory that these are all movements which leave no trace nor the theory that the means of propulsion is mysterious is entirely satisfactory in every case. But there is probably more to it than simply that all these things are mysterious. If the purpose of the author was to set people guessing what is the common element, he has succeeded better than he expected.

The meaning of the last line is uncertain. In any case the word *way* is used here in a different sense from the others, and it may be the element of surprise in this last line which is the real point of the saying. It has been interpreted variously as referring to sexual intercourse, to its result in childbearing, and to the mysterious force which enables a man to obtain a girl's love.

20. Another isolated saying, probably placed here because of its first words, which are the same as the first words of the previous four lines. 'Eating' here may be a euphemism for sexual intercourse, or the point may be the casual unconcern with which the woman moves from bed to board. This is a shrewd comment on the human capacity for dismissing a sense of guilt by rationalizing one's misdeeds.

21–3. The portentous introduction to this series suggests a humorous intention: only the first of the four could possibly be said to be earth-shaking. It is not quite clear what the four have in common. The N.E.B. translators, judging by the way in which they have rendered the passage, think that the point is the intolerable behaviour of certain people when they meet with unexpected good fortune. Alternatively these may simply be examples of astonishing occurrences which upset the divine Order of things, and so are, in a sense, 'earth-shaking'. In that case it would be better to translate *a churl gorging himself* as 'a churl who gets enough to eat' (the point being that churls, being very unpleasant persons, ought to starve) and *a woman unloved when she is married* as 'an unattractive woman who finds a husband'.

24-8. This saying is based on observation of nature, but it also has a didactic purpose: to show that it is wisdom, rather than physical strength, which counts in the climb towards success. The point is similar to that of 16: 32.

27. *in detachments*: the meaning of this word is not certain, but the point is clear: locusts, though tiny, are extremely clever in that they organize themselves very efficiently without even needing a leader.

28. *the lizard* illustrates the point of the saying especially well: it is by its capacity for climbing that it finds itself in the company of kings!

29-31. There is probably no point to this saying beyond the listing of creatures with one common characteristic. The last line is obscure in the Hebrew, and it may be that originally there was a reference here to a fourth animal rather than to the king.

32-3. This saying is very difficult. Verse 32 has the form of an Instruction, and verse 33 purports to give an explanation for it; but the 'explanation' is quite obscure.

32. *fond of filthy talk*: the usual translation of the verb represented by this phrase is '(and) have made wicked plots'.

hold your tongue: literally, 'hand on mouth'. This may mean 'Keep quiet!', as the N.E.B. translators take it, or it may be an adverbial phrase going with the verb: 'if you make plans

with your hand on your mouth' – a reference to secret
intrigue. If this is so, the sentence is incomplete.

33. *provocation leads to strife*: literally, 'the wringing of the
nostrils leads to strife'. This line is very similar in the Hebrew
to the previous line, and may be merely a variant of it. If so
it can be ignored.

nose...blood: these two words can also mean, respectively,
'anger' and 'bloodshed', and there may be a deliberate play on
their meanings, the other meaning being 'the pressure of anger
leads to bloodshed'. If this is in fact the real meaning, the point
may be that the exercise of pressure can produce either good
or bad results according to the circumstances. Anger is dangerous, and should be kept in check. ✷

SECTION VII. PROVERBS 31:1–9

THE SAYINGS OF LEMUEL

Sayings of Lemuel king of Massa, which his mother **31**
taught him:

— What, O my son, what shall I say to you,[a]   2
you, the child of my womb and answer to my prayers?
Do not give the vigour of your manhood to women   3
nor consort with those who make eyes at[b] kings.
It is not for kings, O Lemuel, not for kings to drink 4
wine
nor for princes to crave strong drink;
if they drink, they will forget rights and customs   5
and twist the law against their wretched victims.
Give strong drink to the desperate   6
and wine to the embittered;

[a] what shall I say to you: *prob. rdg., cp. Sept.; Heb. om.*
[b] who make eyes at: *prob. rdg.; Heb. unintelligible.*

7   such men will drink and forget their poverty
    and remember their trouble no longer.
8   Open your mouth and speak up for the dumb,
    against the suit of any that oppose them;
9   open your mouth and pronounce just sentence
    and give judgement for the wretched and the poor.

✻ This is the only example in Proverbs of an Instruction
addressed specifically to a king or young prince giving him
advice on the performance of his duties. There are several such
works from Egypt and Mesopotamia, though this is the only
known example where it is the mother of the young man to
whom the authorship is attributed. Like the Sayings of Agur,
this is non-Israelite wisdom literature. On the location of
Massa see the note on 30: 1.

2. *what shall I say to you*: the Hebrew simply has 'What?'.
An alternative suggestion to the interpretation of the N.E.B.
is that the word translated 'what' is really a rare word meaning
'listen', 'take heed'.

answer to my prayers: literally, 'son of my vows'. The child
had been born in answer to a vow made to God by the mother,
as in the case of Samuel (1 Sam. 1: 11).

3. On women. It was a commonplace of ancient Near
Eastern wisdom literature that it was dangerous for men in
positions of responsibility to become involved with women,
who were believed to be untrustworthy. The legend of the
'beautiful spy' is a very old one!

The second line is unintelligible in the Hebrew: 'nor your
ways to destroy kings'. It is probable that this line originally
contained a thought parallel with that of the first line, and the
N.E.B. translation represents one attempt to restore the original wording.

4-7. On drunkenness. If they are taken literally these verses
prohibit drinking altogether; but such abstemiousness would
have been unheard of in the royal courts of the time. What is

forbidden to kings is more likely to be drunkenness, which muddles the wits and corrupts the character. On the other hand drunkenness is, according to the author, appropriate to the wretched, as it makes them forget their misery.

4. *strong drink*: more precisely, 'beer'.

5. *rights and customs*: kings were not superior to the law in the ancient Near East. In one of the early Egyptian royal instructions, *Merikare*, the king, speaking to his son, makes it clear that it is the duty of a king to maintain justice: 'Do justice while you are on earth;...do not oppress the widow; supplant no man in the property of his father;...be on your guard against punishing unjustly.' Nevertheless the king's position gave him opportunities to *twist* or break *the law*. The Babylonian *Advice to a Prince* gives an impressive catalogue of acts of injustice which the king is liable to commit, together with a list of the corresponding acts of divine retribution which will follow.

6-7. It is difficult to be certain whether these verses are inspired by cynicism or are intended to be taken seriously. The word *Give* in verse 6 is in the plural in Hebrew, and so does not appear to be addressed to King Lemuel personally.

8-9. On justice towards the helpless. The king was the supreme judge, to whom appeals were brought. This judicial function is well illustrated by the stories of Solomon's judgement (1 Kings 3: 16-28) and of the woman of Tekoah (2 Sam. 14: 4-11), in which the king overrules the customary procedures in favour of a poor widow. See also the note on verse 5.

8. *against the suit of any that oppose them*: the Hebrew is not clear here. One alternative translation would be 'for those who suffer the vicissitudes of fortune'. ✳

SECTION VIII. PROVERBS 31: 10–31

A capable wife

10 WHO CAN find a capable wife?
    Her worth is far beyond coral.
11 Her husband's whole trust is in her,
    and children are not lacking.
12 She repays him with good, not evil,
    all her life long.
13 She chooses wool and flax
    and toils at her work.
14 Like a ship laden with merchandise,
    she brings home food from far off.
15 She rises while it is still night
    and sets meat before her household.[a]
16 After careful thought she buys a field
    and plants a vineyard out of her earnings.
17 She sets about her duties with vigour[b]
    and braces herself for the work.[c]
18 She sees that her business goes well,
    and never puts out her lamp at night.
19 She holds the distaff[d] in her hand,
    and her fingers grasp the spindle.
20 She is open-handed to the wretched
    and generous to the poor.
21 She has no fear for her household when it snows,
    for they are wrapped in two cloaks.

[a] *Prob. rdg.; Heb. adds* and a prescribed portion for her maidens.
[b] sets...vigour: *lit.* girds up her loins with strength.
[c] for the work: *so Sept.; Heb. om.*
[d] *Mng. of Heb. word uncertain.*

She makes her own coverings,   22
and clothing of fine linen and purple.

Her husband is well known in the city gate   23
when he takes his seat with the elders of the land.

She weaves linen and sells it,   24
and supplies merchants with their sashes.

She is clothed in dignity and power   25
and can afford to laugh at tomorrow.

When she opens her mouth, it is to speak wisely,   26
and loyalty is the theme of her teaching.

She keeps her eye on the doings of her household   27
and does not eat the bread of idleness.

Her sons with one accord call her happy;   28
her husband too, and he sings her praises:

'Many a woman shows how capable she is;[a]   29
but you excel them all.'

Charm is a delusion and beauty fleeting;   30
it is the God-fearing woman who is honoured.

Extol her for the fruit of all her toil,   31
and let her labours bring her honour in the city gate.

* Although there is no new heading in the text, there can be
no doubt that 31: 10–31 constitutes a complete and independent poem belonging to the type known as 'acrostic', in which
the initial letters of the lines in Hebrew, read vertically from
the top, have a significance of their own. In this case they form
the Hebrew alphabet: the first line in Hebrew (corresponding
to a verse in the N.E.B.) begins with the first letter of the
Hebrew alphabet, *aleph*, the second with the second letter,
beth, and so on through the entire Hebrew alphabet of
22 letters. There are other alphabetic acrostics in the Old
Testament: Ps. 9–10; 25; 119; Lam. 1; 2; 3; 4. Some of these

[a] *Or* Many daughters show how capable they are.

are multiple acrostics, in which several successive lines begin
with the same letter before passing on to the next.

The theme of the poem is the ideal wife seen from a practical and totally unromantic point of view, which is well
summed up in verse 30, which makes it clear that beauty is the
last thing a man should look for in a wife, as in any case it will
not last long! The whole emphasis of the poem is on the
benefits which the wife will bring to her husband and family
by her industry and reliability. Behind it all lies the sense of
importance attached by the ancient Israelite to the welfare and
reputation of the family: material prosperity and good standing in the community go together, and a good wife is necessary to their achievement.

As a comparison of this poem with sayings like 31: 3 shows,
the wisdom literature of the Old Testament had a somewhat
ambivalent, though not necessarily self-contradictory, attitude
towards women. In Proverbs, especially in chapters 1–9, much
is said about women as being untrustworthy and fatal to men's
well-being; yet occasionally, as in this poem and in sayings
like 12: 4; 18: 22; 19: 14, the existence of the good woman is
recognized, while in other sayings the role of the mother is
highly praised. But it is clear that the wisdom writers felt that
such women were hard to come by.

The writer's self-imposed task of beginning each line with a
successive letter of the alphabet evidently presented him with
great difficulties, and the result is that he was unable to establish a consistent sequence of thought. He jumps about from
one thing to another, although everything which he says con-
tributes to the total picture. It has been suggested that the poem
is a handbook for brides; but everything is viewed from the
man's point of view, and it is more likely that it is a handbook
for prospective bridegrooms. It is extremely valuable as a
detailed description of Israelite family life.

10. *Who can find*: this type of question is equivalent to a
statement that something is extremely rare; *beyond coral* has a
similar meaning: see the note on 20: 15. Compare *Papyrus*

Insinger IX 8: 8: 'A woman who manages her household well is irreplaceable riches.'

11. *children*: an alternative translation would be 'profit' (literally, 'spoils' or 'booty').

13. *toils at her work*: alternatively, 'takes pleasure in her work'. Note that although the family is evidently one of considerable social status (verse 23), the Israelite wife did not live in idleness, but made clothes for the family (verses 21–2) and also woven objects for sale (verse 24).

14. This may refer to the use of imported food bought from travelling merchants, but more probably *from far off* refers to additional delicacies which she is able to obtain by trading her own products locally though from further afield than her husband's farm.

15. The third line of this verse has been relegated to a footnote by the N.E.B. translators as a later addition on the grounds that a three-line verse is very improbable in a poem which otherwise consists entirely of two-line verses.

16. Such serious enterprises as the purchase of property were usually reserved for men. It has been suggested that the verse means no more than that the purchase of additional land is made possible by the wife's economies and earnings. On the other hand the expression *After careful thought* seems to indicate that it is she herself who negotiates the purchase

17. The N.E.B. footnote gives the literal translation of this verse. To gird up one's loins is to tuck the skirts of a long robe, whether a man's or a woman's, into the belt to allow freedom of movement in doing heavy work.

18. *never puts out her lamp at night*: whether this is a reference to a custom, still observed by modern Palestinian Arabs, of keeping a lamp burning all night to keep away the power of darkness is uncertain. The burning of a lamp was also a symbol of prosperity, since the poor would be unable to afford it: compare Job 18: 6; Jer. 25: 10. But here, where the context emphasizes the wife's diligence, the expression may simply be a figurative expression like our 'burning the midnight oil'.

19. In simple hand-spinning the *distaff*, which is held in one hand, holds the wool, which is twisted into a thread and wound on to the *spindle* held in the other hand.

21. *two cloaks*: the Hebrew has 'scarlet', which would be a luxury, but not especially useful for keeping out the cold. In the N.E.B. translation a slight alteration of the word has yielded a word meaning 'two', that is, two layers of clothing.

22. *coverings*: that is, 'coverlets' or 'bedspreads'.

23. *the city gate*: see the note on 1: 21. The point here is that the husband is not only one of the prominent citizens or *elders of the land*, who took part in all the discussions and business concerning the city, but *well known* there: in other words, he is a prominent and respected member of that assembly because his wife has greatly enhanced his reputation.

land: this word sometimes appears to mean 'city', and this would be an appropriate translation here.

25. *She is clothed*: for the metaphor compare Ps. 93: 1: 'The LORD is king; he is clothed in majesty.'

26. *loyalty*: this word, which occurs a number of times in Proverbs, has a wide range of meanings. Here it is difficult to be certain whether it is best translated by 'loyalty' or by 'love, kindness'. The role of the mother in teaching her children is also referred to in 1: 8; 6: 20; 31: 1.

29. *Many a woman*: literally, 'daughters' (see the N.E.B. footnote). The word has something of the same meaning here as 'girls' in modern colloquial English.

30. It should not be thought that the ancient Israelites were insensitive to feminine beauty and charm: the raptures of the bridegroom in the Song of Songs are enough to show that this was not so. But the author here is giving advice to a prospective husband; and, like the author of 11: 22, he is concerned to point out that more solid characteristics are necessary for a successful and happy marriage. Compare also Ruth 4: 9–12.

the God-fearing woman: the Hebrew is more precise: 'the woman who fears Yahweh'. This is the only phrase in the poem in which religion is mentioned. The Septuagint has a some-

what different text which suggests the possibility that originally a phrase like the 'capable wife' of verse 10 stood here,
and that the phrase 'who fears Yahweh' was later substituted
for it by someone who believed that the practical skill or
'wisdom' of an excellent wife could only be the consequence
of a firm religious faith. ✷

✷   ✷   ✷   ✷   ✷   ✷   ✷   ✷   ✷   ✷   ✷   ✷   ✷

LIST OF SUBJECTS

This list is not intended to be exhaustive either in its coverage of subjects or in the references under any one subject. It is simply intended to illustrate one approach to the study of Proverbs. Themes such as the inevitability of the ruin of the wicked and the certainty of the prosperity of the righteous, which are reiterated in verse after verse, have not been included because an endless string of references is of no great use to the reader. What is more important is to compare and contrast different treatments of the same theme: this has been the main principle behind the compilation of this list, although in some cases all the examples of a particular type of saying have been given. Themes which occur only once have not been included: this is in no sense an index. It is hoped that the reader will be encouraged by it both to compare the examples given and also to extend the list of themes through his own study of the book.

Animal sayings: 6: 6–8; 30: 15, 18–19, 24–8, 29–31

Bad company, avoidance of: 1: 10–19; 3: 31–2; 4: 14–17; 16: 29; 22: 24–5; 23: 20–1; 24: 1–2

Bribery: 15: 27; 17: 8, 23; 18: 16; 21: 14

Drunkenness: 20: 1; 23: 20–1, 29–35; 31: 4–7

God as seeing and controlling all things: 5: 21; 15: 3, 11; 16: 1–4, 9, 33; 17: 3; 19: 21; 20: 12, 24, 27; 21: 2, 30–1; 22: 2; 24: 12; 29: 13, 26

Justice, the administration of: 17: 15, 23, 26; 18: 5, 17–18; 21: 28

Kings and rulers: 14: 28, 35; 16: 10, 12–15; 19: 12; 20: 2, 8, 26, 28; 21: 1; 22: 11; 23: 1–3; 25: 2–3, 5–7, 15; 29: 4, 12, 14; 31: 1–9

Laziness and hard work: 6: 6–11; 10: 4–5, 26; 12: 11, 24, 27; 13: 4; 15: 19; 19: 15, 24; 20: 4, 13; 21: 25–6; 22: 13; 24: 30–4; 26: 13–16; 28: 19

Numerical sayings: 6: 16–19; 30: 15–16, 18–19, 21–3, 24–8, 29–31

Parents, education, discipline: 1: 1–9; 2: 1; 3: 1–4, 12; 4: 1–5, 10–13, 20–2; 5: 1–2, 7; 6: 20–3; 7: 1–3, 24; 10: 1, 17; 12: 1; 13: 1, 18, 24; 15: 5, 10, 12, 20, 31–3; 17: 21, 25; 19: 13, 18, 25–7; 20: 20, 30; 22: 6, 15; 23: 12–16, 19, 24–6; 28: 7; 29: 1, 3, 15, 17, 19, 21; 30: 11, 17

Quarrels: 3: 30; 10: 12; 15: 18; 18: 18–19; 20: 3; 26: 17, 20–1; 28: 2, 25; 29: 9, 22

Sacrifice: 3: 9–10; 7: 14; 15: 8; 21: 3, 27

Self-control (see also under speech): 11: 12–13; 12: 16, 23; 13: 3; 14: 29; 17: 27–8; 25: 28; 29: 11, 20

Speech, wise and unwise, silence: 10: 8, 11, 14, 18–21, 31–2; 11: 9, 12; 12: 14, 17–19; 13: 3; 14: 3; 15: 1–2, 4, 7, 23; 16: 23–4; 17: 7, 27–8; 18: 20–1; 21: 23; 23: 9; 25: 11; 26: 4–5, 7, 22–8

Standing surety: 6: 1–5; 11: 15; 17: 18; 20: 16; 22: 26–7; 27: 13

Wealth: 10: 2, 15, 22; 11: 4, 18, 24–5, 28; 12: 9; 13: 7–8, 11, 22; 14: 20; 15: 6, 16–17; 16: 8, 16; 17: 1, 16; 18: 11, 23; 19: 1, 4, 6–7; 22: 7; 23: 4–5; 27: 23–7; 28: 6, 8, 20, 22; 30: 8–9

Wisdom, the benefits of: 1: 33; 2: 10–16; 3: 13–18; 4: 6–9; 8: 12–21, 34–6

Wisdom as bride: 4: 6–9; 7: 4

Wisdom and creation: 3: 19–20; 8: 22–31

Wisdom, the infinite value of: 2: 4; 3: 13–18; 4: 7; 8: 10–11; 23: 23

Wisdom as teacher: 1: 20–33; 8: 1–36; 9: 1–6

Women: 2: 16–19; 5: 3–6, 8–20; 6: 24–35; 7: 5–27; 11: 16, 22; 12: 4; 18: 22; 19: 14; 21: 9, 19; 22: 14; 23: 27–8; 25: 24; 27: 15–16; 30: 20; 31: 3, 10–31

A NOTE ON FURTHER READING

A fuller commentary on Proverbs may be found in W. McKane, *Proverbs: A New Approach* (S.C.M. Old Testament Library, 1970), which also contains a detailed study of the Egyptian and Mesopotamian wisdom books. R. B. Y. Scott, *Proverbs and Ecclesiastes* (Doubleday, Anchor Bible, 1965), is also very valuable. A shorter commentary is that of E. Jones (S.C.M. Torch Series, 1961). Among other books which provide background material on the wisdom literature are R. N. Whybray, *Wisdom in Proverbs* and W. McKane, *Prophets and Wise Men*, both published in the S.C.M. Studies in Biblical Theology series in 1965, J. Wood, *Wisdom Literature. An Introduction* (Duckworth, 1967), and R. B. Y. Scott, *The Way of Wisdom* (Macmillan, 1971).

Many more parallels from non-Israelite wisdom literature could have been quoted in the commentary than space permitted. Those readers who wish to read more of this literature will find translations of large sections of most of these works in J. B. Pritchard (ed.), *Ancient Near Eastern Texts Relating to the Old Testament* (Princeton University Press, first published in 1950). The quotations in the commentary are, however, not necessarily taken from this edition.

In the case of some of these works precise references are appended to the quotations in the commentary. Quotations from *Amen-em-opet* and *Papyrus Insinger* are identified by the number of the chapter (where appropriate) in Roman numerals, followed by the numbers of the column and line(s) in Arabic numerals; for *Onchsheshonqy* column and line are given; for *Ahikar* and *Counsels of Wisdom* the line only. For quotations from other works, most of which are fairly short, no references are given for technical reasons; identification should not be difficult.

REFERENCES TO
NON-ISRAELITE LITERATURE

A. Egyptian

The Instruction of the Vizier Ptah-hotep 3–4, 8, 32, 74, 102, 115, 135, 162–3

The Instruction for King Merikare 88, 122, 181

The Kemit 30

The Song of Antef 102

The Wisdom of Ani 25, 46, 102, 148

The Instruction of Amen-em-opet 3, 15, 25, 29, 67, 68, 74, 77, 79, 85, 88, 89, 90, 94, 97, 102, 105, 132–6, 156, 189

Papyrus Insinger 25, 93, 95, 97, 125, 157, 184–5, 189

The Instructions of Onchsheshonqy 89, 136, 189

B. Babylonian and Assyrian

Counsels of Wisdom 33, 114, 122, 148, 189

Advice to a Prince 181

The Words of Ahikar 6, 33, 39, 115, 132, 136, 148, 156, 189

INDEX

Abaddon 89
Absalom 158
Accadian language 7
acrostic poems 183–4
Adonijah 95
adultery, adulteress 22–3, 35–6, 41, 42, 45, 46, 52, 55–6, 83, 125, 177
Agur, Sayings of 171–4
Ahithophel 68
alphabet, Hebrew 183–4
Amos 67
Amos, book of 40, 67, 88
animal sayings 39, 178
animals, concern for 73
Apocrypha 51
Arabia, Arabs 5, 172, 176, 185
Assyria, Assyrians 6, 7; wisdom literature of 5–6; see also Mesopotamia, wisdom literature

Babylonia, Babylonians 7; language of 7; religion of 56; wisdom literature of 5–6, 7, 33, 181; see also Mesopotamia, wisdom literature
blessings and curses 152, 169, 174
borrowing and lending 39, 162
boundary-stones 90
bribery 90, 100, 121, 165

Canaan, Canaanites 6, 7, 23, 64; cities of 5, 7; culture of 5; wisdom literature of 5
Christian teaching 9, 25, 32, 33, 51, 63, 110, 116, 143, 147, 149
Chronicles, first book of 172

city gates 20, 158, 186
Colossians, letter to 51
comparisons 58
Corinthians, first letter to 51
counsellors 68
country life 90, 95, 158–9
court, Judaean 4; wisdom and 68, 100
courtiers 33, 95, 133
creation of the world 27, 51, 52, 85, 93–4, 124

Darda 5
David 4, 5, 12, 50, 85, 95, 117, 158, 159
dead, land of 23, 46, 89–90
death, survival after 62, 70
Death as god 18, 23, 79, 120
death penalty 23
'detestable to the LORD' 29, 67
Deuteronomy, book of 25, 29, 33, 67, 73, 99, 116, 173
discipline, parental 6; divine 25; see also punishment, corporal
drunkenness 137, 138–9, 180–1

Ecclesiastes, book of 116
Ecclesiasticus, book of 51, 109, 164, 173
education 3, 4, 17, 20, 80, 84, 101; Egyptian 4, 80; Israelite 7, 17; parental 17; theories of 1–2, 14, 124, 125; see also schools
Egypt, Egyptians 3, 4, 5, 6, 7, 40, 45, 74, 88; literature of 3, 4, 30, 50, 132; prayer in 163–4; religion of 8, 27, 50, 93;

Egypt *cont.*
  schools in 4, 80; thought of
  102; wisdom literature of 3–5,
  6, 7, 85, 102, 111, 180; *see also*
  schools
epic literature 39
Ethan the Ezrahite 5
Euphrates, valley of 5
Exodus, book of 25, 42, 74, 114,
  115, 137
Ezekiel, book of 1

family, importance of 99–100,
  168, 184, 185
famine 69
father-to-son formula 3–4, 6, 17
fear of the LORD 10, 11, 16, 20,
  23, 91, 94
fertility symbolism 37, 70
forced labour 74
forgiveness 100
friendship 100, 101, 143, 156

Genesis, book of 70, 99, 126,
  172

heart 33, 68, 158
Hebrews, letter to 25
Heman 5
Hezekiah 4, 11, 12, 146
humour 13, 111, 125, 153, 177–8
husband 36, 42, 46, 184–6

imperative form 3–4, 6
incongruous things 109
individual, society and 11, 67, 68,
  104, 140, 156–7, 168
insolent man 20, 55, 77, 125
Instructions 3, 6, 10, 15, 17, 36,
  57, 133, 147; Egyptian 3, 7, 10,
  14, 15, 17, 24, 32, 33, 88, 89,
  135, 136, 138, 181; Israelite

3–5, 14, 17, 19, 20, 35, 44;
  Mesopotamian 33; *see also*
  wisdom literature
Isaiah 10, 85
Isaiah, book of 10, 50, 88, 90, 173
Israel 3, 4, 5, 7, 8, 11, 17, 23, 25,
  39, 64, 76, 95; culture of 3;
  education in 17; history of 6,
  7, 11, 74; laws of 25, 42, 73, 74,
  99, 104, 115; literature of 11,
  146; politics in 9–10; religion
  of 8, 9, 11, 16, 20, 23, 28, 29,
  45–6, 59, 94, 164; society of
  109, 185; thought of 9, 68,
  143, 184; wisdom literature of
  85, 124; wisdom tradition of
  4, 5, 16; *see also* wisdom literature

James, letter of 33
Jeremiah 10,
Jeremiah, book of 25, 185
Jesuits 124
Jesus 156; teaching of 85, 143,
  147
Joab 95
Job, book of 25, 39, 52, 85, 94,
  121, 173, 185
John, Gospel of (fourth Gospel)
  51
Joseph 126
Judah, state of 7, 10, 117, 146,
  159
Judas Iscariot 156
judges 101, 142–3
Judges, book of 16, 169
judgement after death 67
justice, divine 94

Kalcol 5
Kings, first book of 1, 4, 5, 16,
  39, 95, 117, 181

kings 56, 93, 100, 147; accessibility of 2, 170; and law 181; and prophets 10; and taxation 168; and wisdom 15, 50; and wisdom literature 4, 15–6; as agents of God 120; as judges 94–5, 99, 170, 181; authority of 100, 113, 117; divinely given powers of 50, 94–5, 117, 120, 169; duties of 169, 181; inscrutability of 147; Israelite 4, 10, 159, 168

Lamentations, book of 183
lamp, ever-burning 78
Law of Moses (Torah) 51, 162
laws, ancient Near Eastern 67, 168; Israelite 25, 73, 74, 99, 104, 115
legal practice 105, 106, 142–3
Lemuel 12, 172, 179–181
Leviticus, book of 23, 45, 63, 136, 162, 169
life, eternal 67, 89–90; meaning of 63; staff of 78; tree of 70, 78
LORD, name of the 105
lots, casting of 97, 105–6
love, goddess of 50, 56
Luke, Gospel of 147

Maat (goddess of truth) 27, 50
magic 39
Mahol, sons of 5
Malachi, book of 85
marriage 23, 36–7, 110, 184–7
Massa 12, 172
Matthew, Gospel of 32, 63, 73, 85, 110, 143
Mesopotamia 3, 5, 7, 40; culture of 5; literature of 3, 6, 50; religions of 8, 50; wisdom literature of 3, 7, 180; see also Babylonia, Babylonians
Micah 67
mnemonic devices 56
mother, teaching of 17, 186
myth, mythology 18, 23, 51, 70, 78–9, 120

name, importance of 62
narrative form 45, 143
Near East, ancient 7, 15; beliefs of 18, 64, 68, 94–5, 137, 142; ethical codes of 85, 137; kings of 117, 141; laws of 67, 90, 142, 168; literature of 32, 70, 101, 142; poetry of 58; religions of 37, 70, 163; society in 39, 156–7; thought of 33, 57; traditions of 50; wisdom literature of 7, 16, 17, 39, 46, 74, 83, 85, 90, 97, 142, 147, 150, 168
next-of-kin, law of 136
numerical sayings 39–40, 174, 176–9

old age 96–7, 117
onomastica 40
Order, divine 7–8, 18, 20, 27, 64, 74, 93, 117, 126, 149, 178
orthodoxy, Jewish 41, 173

Palestine 5, 148, 149
parallelism, poetical 57–8, 62
parents, reverence for 115, 137, 165, 177
path of life 29, 31–2, 83
Paul 13, 116, 149
Peter 110
poetry 2, 41, 51, 56–9, 164
polytheism 8, 51
poor, kindness to 85, 125–6
poverty 89, 96

prayer 88
prophets 9–10, 13, 20, 67, 90, 94, 101, 168
prostitutes 45, 56
proverbs, descriptive 6, 57, 59; English 1, 78; literary, 2, 3; popular 1–2, 56, 106
Psalms, book of 32, 33, 41, 52, 58, 94, 95, 97, 117, 120, 143, 173, 183, 186
punishment, corporal 6, 80, 110, 117, 136, 169

questions, use of 173

reminiscences, teacher's 30, 45, 143–4
repentance 94, 114
retribution, doctrine of 79–80, 100, 110
riddles 16, 96
Romans, letter to 13, 116, 149
Ruth, book of 186

sacrifice 25, 45–6, 88, 94, 99, 122
Samson 16
Samuel 168, 180
Samuel, first book of 1, 97, 168, 180; second book of 50, 68, 85, 95, 99, 117, 158, 181
schools 7, 17, 19, 36, 80, 100, 114, 123, 158
science 39
scribes 4, 6, 7, 134, 146–7
self-control 83, 85, 97, 102, 149–50
Semitic beliefs 114, 152
Septuagint 29, 30, 52, 64, 68, 84, 104, 109, 117, 120, 124, 125, 142, 153, 161, 163, 171–2, 186
Sermon on the Mount 32
sexual rites 46

Shamash 39
shared offering 45–6
Sheol 18, 36, 46, 158
Shimei 95
silence 102
sins, confession of 163–4
slander 68, 104–5
slaves, slavery 99, 109
Solomon 4, 5, 11, 12, 15–16, 39, 61, 95, 144, 168, 181
Song of Songs 138, 186
speech, proper use of 33, 62–3, 77, 88, 104, 106, 122, 136
spinning 186
spirit, human 93; of God 51
standing surety 38–9, 115
state officials 4, 134
Stupidity, the Lady 54, 55
Sumerians 5–6
Syria 3
Syriac translation 109

table manners 135
taxation 168
Tekoa, woman of 181
temple of Jerusalem 78
Ten Commandments 114, 137
theft 42
troublemakers 39
Two Ways, doctrine of 32, 55, 75

usury 162

vengeance 116
vows 45–6, 116

water as sexual symbol 36–7
wealth 62, 64, 77–8, 95, 105, 115–16, 135, 167
wheel of fortune 116
widows 90

Index

wife, capable 73, 183–6
wisdom, and the court 68; and
creation 27, 50–2; and the
individual 11; and politics
9–10; and prophecy 9–10; as
attribute of God 14, 15, 50–1;
as begotten by God 51; as
bride 30–1, 45, 50; as child 52;
as craftsman 52; as gift of
God 22; as instructress 9, 19,
49; as personal being 9, 14, 19,
26, 51; as possession of God 9,
20, 27, 30; as precious commodity 14, 22, 26; feast of 54;
gifts of 50, 139; house of 52,
54, 82, 139; identified with
Christ 51; practical 8, 9, 14;
pre-existence of 51; self-praise
of 49, 50; tribal 5
wisdom literature 3–5; Arabian
5; Assyrian 5, 6; Babylonian
5, 7; Canaanite 5, 57; Egyptian
3, 5–6, 7, 30, 33, 88; Israelite
(and politics) 9–10, (distinctive character of) 7–11; (religious value of) 7–11, 13,
(scope of) 7, (universality of)

11; Mesopotamian 3, 6, 7;
Sumerian 5; see also Near
East, ancient
Wisdom of Solomon 51
wisdom teachers 18, 89, 110, 113,
124; appeal of 17, 30; as models
for their pupils 137; claims of
19; fees charged by 20, 101;
methods of 77, 144; promises
of 26; reputation of 157; skill
of 138, 144; teaching of (and
sacrifice) 25, (and the Law)
104, 162, (and the Order) 20,
(equated with the fear of the
LORD) 91, (equated with wisdom) 14, 22, 44, 49, 50, (value
of) 45; theories of 124, 125
wisdom tradition, ancient Near
Eastern 3–7; Arabian 5; Egyptian 4; Israelite 4
wise man 12, 89, 172
Word of God 9, 10, 41, 51
work 62, 96, 185

Yahweh (the name) 8

Ziba 99